Longman Resources for Writers

MODEL RESEARCH PAPERS FROM ACROSS THE DISCIPLINES

Fifth Edition

Diane Gould
Shoreline Community College

LONGMAN

An Imprint of Addison Wesley Longman, Inc.

New York • Reading, Massachusetts • Menlo Park, California • Harlow, England
Don Mills, Ontario • Sydney • Mexico City • Madrid • Amsterdam

Model Research Papers from Across the Disciplines, Fifth Edition

CONTENTS

To The Student

Writing a research paper is a common assignment in the college classroom because it gives you an opportunity to use a variety of skills and to engage in independent learning. As you work on your paper, you will practice and demonstrate many of those abilities, including the following:

- focus on a topic and seek relevant information whether you turn to the internet, to books and periodicals in a library, or to interviews with experts and surveys of people in your community;
- read critically, judge the quality of your sources and make useful notes;
- plan a paper that incorporates the information you have discovered and that reflects your own thinking about your topic;
- draft and craft a finished paper, complete with citations in the required format.

Of course, all of these steps contribute to what brings many of you to this page: fear and dread of a lengthy and complex process.

This book is designed to help reduce your stress by showing you how other students like you have developed their research papers and projects. These students have attended different colleges, were at various stages in their work toward associate and bachelor's degrees and wrote in response to assignments that varied in complexity, length, and documentation styles. You'll even find examples of a multimedia paper and a web project that take advantage of computer technology to present information in a nonlinear, hypertext format (links within the paper as well as with other sites on the world wide web), and make use of audio, video, and visual information.

By examining these papers, you'll get an idea of how to handle short, tightly focused papers, longer more fully developed papers, and web-based or multimedia presentations of information. The papers are included as models of typical student work, not as perfect examples of how every paper should look. Each paper includes instructor commentaries on how the paper works and sometimes suggestions for how the writers might have strengthened their work. Finally, each student has written a short description of the process that led to the finished product.

Those who have successfully written research papers before have probably experienced some of the satisfaction of digging deeply into a topic of interest and organizing that learning into a format that can be shared with others. Those who've struggled and those new to this type of assignment are more likely to join the fear and dread crowd, at least initially until some experience leads to increased confidence.

As you read the process essays of each student writer, you'll often see how they turned their anxieties into action, solved the problems they encountered and discovered the pleasures of research and independent learning. As I spoke with student contributors, they were eager to discuss their work, excited about what they had learned and pleased to share their experiences with you.

Their voices offer encouragement and their papers offer models that you can use to glimpse the end result that you're aiming toward. These students worked hard and took pride and satisfaction in their products. You can, too.

Many thanks to the students whose papers appear in this book: Ann Weiss, Cathy DeGrandpre, Adam Hrebeniuk, Janet Ford, Thad Scott, Travis Luken, Peter McMahon, Riley Martin, Tara Tuckwiller, Mike Sill, Tami Kyle, and James McElroy, Jr.

Diane Gould
Shoreline Community College

TEN RESEARCH PAPER REMINDERS

1. MAKE ANXIETY PRODUCTIVE

It is quite common to feel anxious about writing a research paper. Besides being anxious about writing in general, many students feel that they do not know how to plan or do the research for a research paper. Even minor things such as how to quote and document sources often become huge stumbling blocks.

The important thing is not to let your anxiety lead to procrastination. Doing a research paper can be accomplished more easily if you divide it into stages—then you can limit your worries to one isolated task at a time. For example, do not worry about the format of the "Works Cited" or "References" page before you even begin researching. Just make sure you write down the relevant publication information as you research. You can write citations in the specific format when your paper is fully drafted.

The first stage of the research paper might not be the expected outlining or researching a list of books in the library. More likely, you will begin with some informal writing. For instance, write everything you already feel you know about your topic. Do this as free-writing, as a brainstormed list, or as a series of fragments. Set yourself a time goal—see if you can write steadily for 30 minutes, then another 30 minutes. Or set yourself a page goal—try to write three pages, or more. What this preliminary writing can do is show you how much you already know. Often, it can suggest a focus and direction for your research. Mainly, though, it will help boost your confidence. You can write.

2. UNDERSTAND THE ASSIGNMENT

Many students jump into the project without carefully reading the assignment. One of your stages of research might be to write a paraphrase of the assignment, including any questions you have about it. Discuss this paraphrase with your teacher to be sure you have understood the assignment. Keep in mind that there are many levels of complexity and guidelines for how to develop and structure a documented paper. You will need to be sure you understand exactly what you're being asked to do.

This book contains samples of some straightforward information papers, some longer critical papers, and two media-based projects. No matter what the requirements of the assignments, however, all of the papers share a need for accurate use of information and careful attention to documentation guidelines.

3. FIND A CLEAR PURPOSE FOR THE WRITING

If an assignment seems dry and uninteresting to you, find a way to make it interesting. Find an angle from which you could discuss the topic in a new, surprising way. Or find an aspect of the topic that touches on your life in some way. Your preliminary writing may suggest such a focus. Once you have a focus, you also have direction. For example, Mike Sill discovered that his interest in the legal troubles of Microsoft extended to the main topic of the assignment as well.

4. CONSIDER PRIMARY AS WELL AS SECONDARY SOURCES

The difference between a mediocre paper and a really good one is often a matter of primary research. Primary research--interviews, questionnaires, surveys, experiments, personal observation, and original documents--can make a paper very lively for both the writer and the reader. In his case study on telecommuting, James McElroy uses an interview and observation to illustrate and question the secondary research he finds. This turns a potentially dry review-of-the-literature paper into an intriguing picture of a recent work-style.

5. LET YOURSELF BE GUIDED BY YOUR RESEARCH

Beginning with a "thesis" that you must find research to support will almost certainly frustrate you. It is better to begin with a "research question" (or questions) and see what answers you find. Often the research will take you in a direction that is slightly or even radically different from your expectations. In her process writing, Tami Kyle writes that her original idea was to find the studies done on gender-based differences in spatial ability and then just describe them. She didn't expect to find that the studies disagreed with each other or that they were biased toward men. She let her discovery determine an organization for the paper.

6. PLAN TO DRAFT AND REVISE

Merely writing an outline and then filling it in with quotes will not result in a good paper. Moreover, this approach, though it may seem to be the easiest way to write the paper, may very well end up taking a longer time to do than the drafting/revising approach because your ideas and the quotes you find may be difficult to force into a rigid format. Remember that drafts do not have to be perfect; introductions, conclusions, transitions, and grammar corrections can be added at later stages. While doing the first draft or drafts, try to write as much as you can, not as well as can.

7. BE AWARE OF WRITING TO A READER

As you write your drafts, imagine that you're addressing a particular person (someone other than your teacher) or group of people. Consider who would most benefit from reading your paper. This will help you determine tone and vocabulary. In her paper on the editing of the Declaration of Independence, Ann Weiss indirectly addresses the scholar who says that the editing by Congress damaged the Declaration's effectiveness-she wants to show him that he's wrong. In her medical science paper, Tami Kyle is addressing people who do not have specialized knowledge of her subject; hence, she is careful to keep technical terminology to a minimum.

8. GET FEEDBACK WHILE DRAFTING

Get suggestions for revision from other students, from your teacher, or from the writing center. Read your draft aloud so that you can listen to the rhythm of your sentences—sentences that make you gasp for air can be divided, sentences that are all too short can be combined, sentences that all use the same order of sentence parts can be rearranged, etc. More importantly, though, ask your listeners how they hear your paper--are any parts unclear to them? What parts do they like best, and why? What questions do they have about the content?

9. USE CONSISTENTLY THE DOCUMENTATION SYSTEM YOU CHOOSE

There are three primary formats for writing research papers; the MLA (Modern Language Association), the APA (American Psychological Association), and the CBE (Council of Biology Editors) systems. MLA is the system most familiar to students because it is the system used for writing English and Humanities papers. However, if your major is in the social sciences or "hard" sciences, you will find that your teachers will expect you to use one of the other systems. All systems ask that you provide the same author and publication information with your paper; however, the format differs slightly from system to system. Your writer's handbook will discuss all three of these systems, but most likely only the MLA system will be presented in detail. The library, however, should have copies of the most recent complete guidelines for all documentation style. Style guides can also be found on the World Wide Web by simply searching for the style name.

Chicago and Columbia Online styles are also illustrated in this book. Chicago Style is sometimes called the Turabian or Humanities Style and uses superscript numerals and documentary footnotes on related pages. Columbia Online Style provides new guidelines for citations of electronic sources and is illustrated in Thad Scott and Travis Luken's multimedia project.

2

10. EDIT AND PROOFREAD

If you have a spellchecker, use it, but don't rely on it alone. Spellcheckers only catch spelling mistakes, a relatively minor category of possible errors. Read your paper slowly, preferably aloud, to catch other errors. Some students read the paper backwards--last page first, second-to-last page, and so forth--because it distances them from their familiarity with the content that might make it easy to overlook errors. And, of course, check your documentation format against the style guidelines.

Grammar checkers can be useful in calling your attention to long sentences that may need to be divided up and to words and phrases in your text that may lead to a lack of clarity such as the passive voice. Use grammar checker messages as a way to reconsider sentence structure.

Process Writing for "The Editing of the Declaration of Independence"

The assignment for which I wrote this paper asked us to find a text--a story, poem, or essay--for which we could also find an earlier version or even just the author's commentary on writing the piece. We were then to compare the published version with the earlier version or commentary. We were to let the comparison suggest a question about revision, a question that we could then use as a central focus of the paper.

The assignment at first seemed easy. I had read a lot of poetry, and I thought I could just go find a poem by a favorite poet, check out any biographies, autobiographies, or--if really lucky a facsimile draft of a poem--and then write a basic comparison paper, going through the poem line by line. But the more I thought about doing the assignment this way, the more boring it seemed. I had already done many poem "explications," and I felt that my approach to the assignment was leading me right toward yet another explication.

So, I decided to find a text that would not be the usual standard literary work. The idea of the Declaration of Independence came to me during a history class. The professor said something about Jefferson being given the "assignment" of drafting the Declaration, and an image popped into my head of Jefferson as a typical college student--putting off the assignment until the night before it was due, writing all night, then getting the draft torn to pieces during the draft workshop. I began to wonder if Jefferson's draft was subjected to a workshop sort of process.

To my surprise, I not only found the draft of the Declaration, but I also discovered that scholars had already written about it. I knew I had found my topic.

The question about revision was also given to me by the people who had already written about the Declaration. I realized that, since they didn't all agree, I could write my comparison based mainly on the scholars' analyses and secondarily on the draft and final version of the Declaration itself. Once I had my question and my general format in mind, writing the paper was quite easy.

Ann Weiss

The Editing of the Declaration of Independence:

Better or Worse?

By

Ann Weiss

English 101
Professor E. Gonzales

15 May 1994

Paragraph 1

Ann's first paragraph sets forth the problem--a disagreement among scholars about the effectiveness of Congress' revisions to Jefferson's draft of the Declaration of Independence. Ann presents the scholarly disagreement as a literary question about revision and the rhetorical effect of language. Ann's choice of a political document, rather than a work of literature, to illustrate a literary problem gives her paper added interest.

Paragraph 2

Here, Ann summarizes the historical background in order to establish the context.

Paragraphs 1-2

Ann is using the standard Modern Language Association (MLA) in-text citation style. After her paraphrases of material from outside sources, she includes in parentheses the name of the author and the page number(s) on which the material appears. MLA style requires only the author's name and page number(s)--you do not need to include a comma or "p." between name and page number. The period for the sentence follows the citation.

Since Ann cites two references to Wills, the second immediately after the first, she does not need to repeat the author's name in the second citation.

Paragraph 3

The information referred to in the first sentence of this paragraph is mentioned by two sources, so Ann includes both in her citation and separates them by a semicolon.

Paragraph 4

Ann zeros in on the main disagreement, giving her paper a clear focus. Note that she summarizes the main points of the passage, the points that repeat and reinforce the information she provides in paragraph 2.

The Editing of the Declaration of Independence:
Better or Worse?

The Declaration of Independence is so widely regarded as a statement of American ideals that its origins in practical politics tend to be forgotten. The document drafted by Thomas Jefferson was intensely debated in the Continental Congress and then substantially revised before being signed. Since then, most historians have agreed that Jefferson's Declaration was improved in the process. But Jefferson himself was disappointed with the result (Boyd 37); and recently his view has received scholarly support. Thus it is an open question whether the Congress improved a flawed document or damaged an inspired one. An answer to the question requires understanding the context in which the Declaration was conceived and examining the document itself.

The Continental Congress in 1776 was attended by representatives of all thirteen colonies. The colonies were ruled more-or-less separately by Great Britain and had suffered repeated abuses at the hands of King George III, the British Parliament, and local appointed governors. To end the abuses of the British, many colonists were urging three actions: forming a united front, seceding from Britain, and taking control of their own international trade and diplomacy (Wills 325-26). They saw the three actions as dependent on each other, and all three were spelled out in a resolution that was proposed in the Congress on June 7, 1776 (326-27).

The Congress named a five-man committee to prepare a defense of this resolution in order to win the support of reluctant colonists and also to justify secession to potential foreign allies (Malone 219; Wills 330-31). Jefferson, the best writer on the committee, was assigned to draft the document. The other committee members made a few minor changes in his draft before submitting it to the Congress. The Congress made many small and some quite large alterations before approving the document on July 4 (Becker 171).

The most interesting major change, because of the controversy it ultimately generated, was made in Jefferson's next-to-last paragraph. (See Figure 1 for Jefferson's version with the Congress's editing.) Jefferson made several points in the paragraph: the colonists had freely submitted to the British king but not to the British parliament; they had tried repeatedly and unsuccessfully to gain the support of the British people for their cause; yet the British ("unfeeling brethren") had not only ignored the colonists' pleas but also worsened their difficulties by supporting the Parliament. These actions, Jefferson concluded,

Paragraph 5

Ann summarizes the arguments of the main scholars on one side of the debate about this passage in Jefferson's draft. Because Ann mentions the names of the scholars in the text itself, she does not need to include them in the parenthetical citation.

Note that the quotations from these scholars are embedded; that is, they are included within Ann's own prose. Embedding quotes helps the prose read more smoothly and naturally.

Note also the use of brackets in line six. Ann has added the words "the delegates'" and enclosed them in squared brackets [ ] to clarify the meaning of "their" for the reader. Anything you add to a quotation should be likewise enclosed in brackets.

Paragraph 6

Ann brings in the main dissenter in the debate. She devotes an entire paragraph to Wills in order to set him apart from the others in the minds of the readers.

gave the colonists no choice but to separate from England. The Congress cut Jefferson's paragraph by almost two-thirds, leaving only the points about the colonists' appeals to the British, the refusal of the British to listen, and the need for separation.

Until recently, most historians accepted all the Congress's changes in the Declaration as clear improvements. Dumas Malone, author of the most respected biography of Jefferson, expresses "little doubt that the critics strengthened" the Declaration, "primarily by deletion" (222). Julian Boyd, a historian of the period and the editor of Jefferson's papers, observes that "it is difficult to point out a passage in the Declaration, great as it was, that was not improved by their [the delegates'] attention" (36). Carl Becker, considered an expert on the evolution of the Declaration, agrees that "Congress left the Declaration better than it found it" (209). These scholars make few specific comments about the next-to-last paragraph. Becker, however, does say that Jefferson's emphasis on the British Parliament is an allusion to a theory of government that is assumed in the rest of the document, so that the paragraph "leaves one with the feeling that the author, not quite aware that he is done, is beginning over again" (211-12).

The agreement in favor of the Congress's changes was broken in 1978 when the journalist and humanities scholar Garry Wills published a detailed defense of Jefferson's original, particularly his next-to-last paragraph. According to Wills, "Jefferson's Declaration of Independence is a renunciation of unfeeling brethren. His whole document was shaped to make that clear" (319). The British people had betrayed the colonists both politically (by supporting the intrusive Parliament) and emotionally (by ignoring the colonists' appeals), and that dual betrayal was central to Jefferson's argument for secession (303). Wills contends that in drastically cutting the next-to-last paragraph, "Congress removed the heart of his argument, at its climax"(319).

Figure I

Figures can be photocopied texts, maps, drawings, etc. pasted into the paper, or they can be typed along with the paper, as Ann has done here. A different typeface (if one is available), single spacing, or a border around the figure will help to set it off from the rest of the paper.

Materials can also be scanned onto a disk for inclusion in a paper or they can be copied and pasted from online sources. Sources for these images should be noted.

Figures are often explained in the main text of the paper, but in some cases, as in Ann's paper, the figures are complex enough to warrant an explanatory caption. Double-space captions for figures and begin the caption with the abbreviation "Fig."

Nor have we been wanting in attentions to our British

brethren. we have warned them from time to time of attempts ——————— an unwarrantable

by their legislature to extend^ *[a]* jurisdiction over ^ ——

[these our states.] we have reminded them of the circum- ——————— us.

stances of our emigration & settlement here, *[no one of*

which could warrant so strange a pretension: that these

were effected at the expence of our own blood & treasure,

unassisted by the wealth or the strength of Great Britain:

we had adopted one common king, thereby laying a foundation

for perpetual league & amity with them: but that submission

to their parliament was no part of our constitution, nor ever ——————— have

in idea, if history may be credited: and,] we ^appealed to ——————— and we have

their native justice and magnanimity ^*[as well as to]* the ——————— conjured them by

ties of our common kindred to disavow these usurpations which —————— would inevitably

^ *[were likely to]* interrupt our connection and correspondence.

they too have been deaf to the voice of justice & of consan-

guinity, *[and when occasions have been given them, by the*

regular course of their laws, of removing from their councils

the disturbers of our harmony, they have, by their free election,

re-established them in power at this very time too they are

permitting their chief magistrate to send over not only souldiers

of our common blood, but Scotch &foreign mercenaries to invade

& destroy us. these facts have given the last stab to agonizing

affection, and manly spirit bids us to renounce for ever these

unfeeling brethren. we must endeavor to forget our former love

for them, and to hold them as we hold the rest of mankind enemies

in war, in peace friends. we might have been a free and a great

people together; but a communication of grandeur & of freedom it

seems is below their dignity. be it so, since they will have it.

the road to happiness & to glory is open to us too. we will tread —————— we must therefore

it apart from them, and] ^acquiesce in the necessity which ————— and hold them as we

denounces our *[eternal]* separation^ ! hold the rest of mankind

enemies in war,

in peace friends.

Fig. 1: Next-to-last paragraph of the Declaration of Independence, from Jefferson (318-19). 'The text is Jefferson's as submitted by the five-man committee to the Continental Congress. The Congress deleted the passages that are in italics and added the passages in the margin.

Paragraph 7

This is a crucial paragraph because it presents Ann's own position in the debate. While she does not set herself entirely against Wills--a good choice because it makes her appear rational and moderate--she clearly aligns herself with the earlier scholars.

Paragraph 8

Here, Ann takes phrases directly from Jefferson's draft (Figure 1) to illustrate what she is saying about Jefferson's "overheated" and "pouting" tone. The quotations efficiently explain Ann's point to the readers.

Paragraphs 9-10

Ann now presents her reasons for aligning herself with the scholars who say that Congress' revisions made the Declaration of Independence better. Note that she does not merely state her reasons without backing them up with explanations and examples from the passage. The phrases that Ann includes help her show, rather than just tell, that the revisions were effective.

As an explanation of Jefferson's intentions, Will's presentation is convincing. However, a close examination of the original and edited versions of the next-to-last paragraph supports the opinions of earlier historians rather than Wills's argument that the Declaration was damaged by the Congress. The paragraph may have expressed Jefferson's intentions, but it was neither successful in its tone nor appropriate for the purposes of the Congress as a whole.

Part of Jefferson's assignment "was to impart the proper tone and spirit" to the Declaration (Malone 221). He did this throughout most of the document by expressing strong feelings in a solemn and reasonable manner. But in the next-to-last paragraph Jefferson's tone is sometimes overheated, as in the phrases "invade & destroy us," "last stab to agonizing affection," and "road to happiness & to glory." At other times Jefferson sounds as if he is pouting, as in "we must endeavor to forget our former love for them" and "a communication of grandeur & of freedom it seems is below their dignity." Wills comments that critics have viewed this paragraph as resembling "the recollections of a jilted]over" (313). Wills himself does not agree with this interpretation of the tone, but it seems accurate. All the quoted passages were deleted by the Congress.

More important than the problem in tone is the paragraph's inappropriateness for the purposes of the Declaration as the Congress saw them. Specifically, the paragraph probably would not have convinced reluctant colonists and potential foreign allies of the justice and logical necessity of secession. The Congress needed the support of as many colonists as possible, but many colonists still felt strong ties to their friends and relatives in England (Becker 127-28; Boyd 31-32). They would probably have been unhappy with phrases such as "renounce forever" and "eternal separation" that threatened a permanent break in those ties. The Congress deleted those phrases, and it also gave greater stress to Jefferson's one hint of a possible reconciliation with the British: "We must ... hold them as we hold the rest of mankind enemies in war, in peace friends." This thought was moved by the Congress from inside the paragraph to the very end, where it strikes a final note of hope.

The Congress also strengthened the appeal of the Declaration to potential allies, who would have needed assurance that the colonists were acting reasonably and cautiously. Both Jefferson's and the Congress's

Paragraph 11

Ann concludes with a paragraph that neatly re-emphasizes her point without tediously summarizing her entire paper. With a research paper this short, a summary conclusion is not necessary as readers can be expected to keep track of the paper's contents.

Overall Comment

Ann's paper shows a clear, narrowly defined focus that not only helps her to keep the paper concise, but also keeps the paper moving along at a quick but natural pace. Although the focus is limited, the implication is that her argument can be extended to the Declaration of Independence as a whole. This decision allows Ann to be very detailed in her paper, rather than trying to make general points about the entire Declaration. It also makes her argument easy to follow and easy to take a stance toward.

It can be argued that Ann's essay is unnecessarily simple. Though it suits the purposes of the assignment very well, Ann could have made her essay more complex by extending her paper in any of several directions. For example, she could have gone on to speculate on the effectiveness of the Declaration of Independence as a whole; she could have brought in more of the historical context to show even more clearly how the word choices affected the Declaration's audiences; or she could have raised questions about the nature of revision or political rhetoric in general. Directions such as these can deepen the discussion and as a result enhance the significance of the paper.

versions note that the colonists often "warned" and "reminded" the British and "appealed to their native justice & magnanimity," but that the British were "deaf to the voice of justice & consanguinity" and left the colonists no choice besides "separation." However, Jefferson buried these statements in lengthy charges against the British, while the Congress stripped away the charges to emphasize the colonists' patience in exploring all avenues of redress and their reluctance in seceding. Instead of "beginning over again" as Becker says Jefferson's version seems to do, the revised paragraph clearly provides the final rational justification for the action of the colonists. At the same time, it keeps enough of Jefferson's original to remind the audience that the colonists are feeling people, motivated by their hearts as well as by their minds. They do not secede enthusiastically but "acquiesce in the necessity" of separation.

Though the Declaration has come to be a statement of this nation's political philosophy, that was not its purpose in 1776. Jefferson's intentions had to bow to the goals of the Congress as a whole to forge unity among the colonies and to win the support of foreign nations. As Boyd observes, the Declaration of Independence "was the result not just of Jefferson's lonely struggle for the right phrase and the telling point, but also of the focusing of many minds—among them the best that America ever produced" (38).

Documentation Format

Ann uses the Modern Language Association (MLA) documentation system. The sources quoted, paraphrased or summarized within the paper are included on a "Works Cited" page. Use the following general rules as a guide in formatting this page:

- Start a new page for "Works Cited."
- Number the page in the same format as the other pages in the paper.
- Center the heading "Works Cited."
- Double-space all lines, and indent the second and subsequent lines of each citation by one-half inch.
- Underline titles of books and periodicals; use quotations marks around titles of articles.
- Alphabetize by main author's last name.
- Sequence the information as follows: author's name, title of article or chapter, title of book or journal, place of publication, publisher, year of publication, and for articles or sections of longer works, the page numbers. Page numbers are not necessary for books.

Font and Layout

This manuscript was produced on a home computer, in 10-point Times font, a popular, professional-looking font suitable for academic publications. The paper is double-spaced, with one-inch margins. The text is flush left, ragged right. Use of the computer allows Weiss to use italics effectively, as opposed to underlining on an older-style typewriter.

Works Cited

Becker, Carl. The Declaration of Independence: A Study in the History of Political Ideas. New York: Knopf, 1956.

Boyd, Jilian P. The Declaration of Independence: The Evolution of a Text. Princeton: Princeton UP, 1945.

Jefferson, Thomas. "Notes of the Proceedings in the Continental Congress." The Papers of Thomas Jefferson. Ed. Julian P.

Boyd et al. Vol. 1. Princeton: Princeton UP, 1950-74. 21 vols.

Malone, Dumas. Jefferson the Virginian. Boston: Little, 1948. 6 vols.

Wills, Garry. Inventing America: Jefferson's Declaration of Independence. Garden City: Doubleday, 1978.

Process Writing for "Beyond the Words: Diversity in American English"

In this assignment, we were to research, discuss and finally take a stand on the English-Only issue being debated in the media, schools and courts of the U.S., and of course, to write persuasively. Since this is a topic that has been passionately and convincingly argued both ways, and since class discussions were equally polarized, I decided to take a few steps back from those arguments. When I write, my greatest challenge is overcoming the blank page. Once some words appear, though, I relish the organizing and rewriting, allowing the essence of the essay to emerge.

After I had researched and listened and discerned my own perspectives about this issue, I realized that my strongest opinion was related to what was missing in all the arguments—mutual respect. I began by questioning the concept of ownership of a language by any one group, and questioning therefore, the right to control it. My plan was to demonstrate that language comes from life, and that American life is good because of, not in spite of, its complicated, ambiguous nature. Then I looked everywhere for simple, non-threatening examples of this complexity and found far too many to include. Building on the simpler concepts I progressed to the weightier ones of race and ethnicity, and the consequences of exclusion. Ultimately, I did not want my arguments just to bolster one or the other side of this issue, but to go back and shake the roots of both.

Working on this assignment and others like it has both broadened and sharpened my thinking on diversity issues, as well as my writing skills. I find that opinions on the diversity of American culture serve well as lenses through which to view current events, history and literature.

Riley Martin

Because this paper is relatively short and informal, there is no outline, table of contents or title page. The double-spaced identification of the writer, the course, the college and the date at the top left corner are all that are needed.

Riley's paper is an example of a short, documented, persuasive essay that has been written for a general audience, a type common in English composition courses. She uses external sources (documented in MLA style) as well as personal experience and reasoning to reinforce the arguments that she makes. The paper has a personal and informal tone that results from the use of the first person and references to the writer's own life.

Paragraph 1
In the opening paragraph, Riley describes the cultural diversity of the nation and connects that plurality to the linguistic diversity inherent in the English language. She links these comments together as she points out that language meets the cultural needs of its speakers. The reader can then infer that pluralism and change in language are natural in a pluralistic society. By this means she sets forth the overall structure of her paper. She attempts to draw the reader into her view by the use of the first person plural pronoun, "we."

Paragraph 2
Riley begins the body of her essay by providing some historical grounding for her discussion. She points out that the break from British English spellings represented in the first American English Dictionary is a corollary to American political independence. She adds that encounters with new situations give rise to new vocabulary. The addition of a few examples of common words borrowed from Native American languages would strengthen her point. Her brief allusion to changing social customs paves the way for her later discussion of etiquette.

Riley Martin

English 102

Professor M.C. Jenkins

Spring, 1996

Beyond the Words: Diversity in American English

The motto of the United States of America, E Pluribus Unum means out of many, one. But one what? Valid points are made on both sides of the English Only debate, of course, but I have yet to hear an argument for English as the official language of the United States that respectfully acknowledges the pluribus (many) part of our motto. A surge of resistance, the urge to protect what we love, or what is familiar, is an understandable first reaction to what appear to be efforts to dilute, bastardize, or submerge so vital and intimate a possession as our language. But to whom does "our" language belong? The evolution of American English into a rich expression of our culture is, upon even a casual inspection, a drama of sorts. The English we defend is a testament to the multicultural nature of the United States. Native speakers of the languages some would like to stamp out have contributed some of their best to American English, and they are not the only groups to have done so. A broader definition of American is required for a just solution to the language debate. Beneath the words and structure of American English, we are inventing, defining and expressing our collective and individual selves. Our American culture is evolving as we speak.

The adolescent British colonies of North America fought the Revolutionary War for the freedom to invent themselves. Among many more consequential outcomes, they changed the spellings of some English words (colour to color, favour to favor, theatre to theater, etc.), and invented many new ones. The word presidential did not exist until the U.S. had a need for it. Webster's dictionary was written to help immigrants to the U.S. with the spelling, and especially the pronunciation of American English words (as opposed to the British version). Some rules of etiquette were also revised in the revolutionaries' efforts to symbolize and ritualize their freedom. Our complicated system of wielding a knife and fork is one such example. British table manners are infinitely less contrived, but we were determined to separate ourselves, even in trivial ways. As the United States spread across the continent, each new territory, more and more distant from its source, took on its own character, which then asserted itself on

Paragraph 3

In this paragraph, Riley points out the additions to the language that have come through non-English speaking immigrants. The emphasis on foods and holidays creates a sense of familiarity with her point in the reader, who is invited to view these vocabulary additions with pride. She reinforces the inclusive tone maintained from the start.

To deepen the argument, Riley could also include examples of words that are less obviously from other languages, but equally common in English.

Paragraph 4

Riley then addresses the fears that people sometimes feel when they cannot understand the speech of others. She chooses the familiar example of teenage slang as a way to make her point in a non-threatening way and emphasizes that most teens outgrow their propensity for slang. By this strategy, she seeks to show the reader that even native English speakers use language that is unfamiliar to other native speakers, indirectly reducing the tendency to look toward second language speakers as the source of "the problem."

Paragraph 5

At this point, Riley returns to the issue of etiquette to underscore how social changes engender linguistic changes that are unlikely to go away, even if they do make some people uncomfortable. She makes it clear that the social conditions of 1984 have changed greatly and points out that the advice offered in the early 80s about language applied to women's issues no longer obtains. She argues at this point for an acceptance of change as normal and necessary, paving the way for her final set of examples, which are much more closely associated with prejudice and the English Only movement.

the language. Different climates, terrain and occupations required new words to express new experiences.

No living language stands still however much we might wish at times that it would. Concentrations of people with common ancestry inevitably included words and expressions from their first language in their use of English. Many of those words have been in common usage for decades or longer. I would not want to try to get along without <u>Irish stew</u>, <u>filet mignon</u>, <u>hors d'oeuvres</u>, <u>chow mien</u>, <u>minestrone</u>, <u>tortilla</u> or Seattle's beloved <u>espresso</u> and <u>croissants</u>. Aren't we all on the town for <u>Cinco de Mayo</u>, <u>Mardi Gras</u> and St. Patrick's Day? These additions to English reflect cultural changes, people working with the tools at hand to define and express themselves. The "official" language must accommodate all of us. This evolution indicates forward motion; it is something in which we can, if we choose, take great pride.

One of the least threatening examples of people trying to define themselves uniquely while making a statement about the majority language's inability to accommodate them is the slang of teenagers. Their customized language can vary greatly from group to group depending on their life experience and the degree to which they feel excluded. I listen intently to my son and his friends defining their experience. <u>Plag,</u> for example, is an adjective, with the very same meaning as <u>dorky</u>, <u>unhip</u>, <u>out-of-style</u>, unfashionable. None of the other words, though, quite captures what his group, in his time, means to express. <u>Doe</u>, an adjective, means <u>good.</u> The adjective <u>booty</u>, on the other hand, is negative. <u>Booty</u>, some will remember, was youth slang years ago, but as a noun (a body part, actually) and with more positive connotations. Young people customize the tools of communication they inherit. This is brilliant since as it increases the tools' usefulness, they are customizing themselves, as well. Yet, this hallmark of youth does not frighten us; we trust they will grow out of this stage.

Women of all races, too, have slowly and at great personal cost, forced American English to yield to their realities. The 14th edition of *Emily Post's Etiquette* is considered by many to be the bible of manners. Ms. Post states, "Ms has no meaning (other than manuscript) and...the only possible pronunciations are either unattractive or unwieldy. I recommend avoiding it...except for a woman who is living with a man and is neither married or single" (17). Luckily, most of us do not consult Emily Post as often as we consult our own sense of what works for us. The courtesy titles traditionally allowed women

21

Paragraph 6

In this penultimate paragraph, Riley gets to the heart of her argument. She makes the point that language variety related to cultural heritage and race is a fact, albeit one feared by many. She uses a quote from James Baldwin as an eloquent addition to her argument and concentrates on the fear that underlies the English Only movement. She focuses on the futility of attempting to regulate language as an ineffective solution that arises from fear and prejudice. She offers an alternative view that values diversity as she moves into her concluding paragraph.

Paragraph 7

In this paragraph, Riley acknowledges the need in every society for clear communication among its citizens and respectful acknowledgement of our differences. She uses a quotation from Martin Luther King, Jr. to underscore her point and wraps up her discussion deftly and succinctly, suggesting the possible outcome of the adoption of her point of view.

do not serve the reality of family structures and business life today. Whether Ms. Post agrees with it or not, Ms. lives. Women added the word feminism to the language of freedom when none other would serve. The expressions palimony, single parent, and latch key children were incorporated to describe new situations. Old words took new or additional meanings: partner and significant other, for example. As the roles of women, and the definition of family expanded, it became necessary to invent and reinvent words to describe American life. American English must evolve to make possible the inclusion of all of the diverse experience of the people of America. While some perceive the feminist movement to be threatening to the fabric of society, I doubt many believe women eventually will outgrow their cause.

Will the Native, African and Hispanic Americans mature past their need to make the language accommodate their experience? We have no reason to believe so. Nor will Asian Americans or new immigrants grow out of their desire to assure, sometimes by operating their own schools, that their children will carry forth their heritage. James Baldwin, in his essay "Black English" says, "People evolve a language in order to describe and thus control their circumstances or in order not to be submerged by a reality they cannot articulate" (184). Currently, one third of the American people do not trace their roots to Europe. Some Americans of European descent are already experiencing what it means to be a minority. No wonder our knee-jerk reaction is fear. Americans accustomed to the privilege afforded majority groups fear the indignities, isolation and prejudice minorities have endured. Efforts to control, or energy spent judging the multicultural nature of the U.S. or the evolution of American English will not keep these changes in the ethnic balance of the population from occurring. What we can do, however, is change the way we feel about our multicultural society. We can learn to value it.

Our instinct to protect what we know and understand, and to fear the unknown, often serves our needs—mindless instinct also serves the other animals. I think we should remember, as well, that many things set us apart from the other animals; our ability to choose is at the top of the list. We can choose to acknowledge the positive value of our diversity. Reverend Martin Luther King, Jr. said, "A riot is at bottom the language of the unheard" (127). It would serve us all to accommodate in our definition of American, the voices of all those who make their homes here. A thoughtful look at the evolution of the American English we love and defend might provide clues to a just answer to our "official language" question. The

Overall Comment

Riley's essay is balanced and strategically effective. Her rhetorical strategy of including the reader in her assertions through the use of the first person plural pronoun helps the reader identify with her point of view. She moves from commonly held ideals to commonly held prejudices and skillfully argues for unity in language through repsect for and appreciation of diversity.

Her uses of sources serves not so much as evidence as it does to call upon familiar voices of authority to reinforce and restate the main points she is making.

need to maintain a standard of language through which we can make ourselves understood in government, business and literature internationally is legitimate. The need and moral obligation to encourage the evolution of an English language as well as the respectful acknowledgment of the importance of other languages that effectively capture and allow expression of our American experience are not so easily met. If we Americans were to actually become who our Constitution says we are, those who do not speak English may just be inspired to learn.

Documentation Format

Riley has chosen MLA style documentation, which is commonly used in the humanities. She has used in-text parenthetical citations, which refer the reader to a short "Works Cited" page. The "Works Cited" list is alphabetized, uses hanging indentation, is double-spaced within and between entries, and uses italics rather than underlining for book titles. Technically only works that are actually cited in the paper should appear on a "Works Cited" list. The final citation in Riley's list could, therefore, be omitted.

Font and Layout

This paper is written using 10-point Arial, a non-serif typeface often accepted in college classes for its readability. The manuscript is double-spaced, with one-inch margins, flush left, ragged right.

Works Cited

Baldwin, James. "On Black English." *About Language.* 4th ed. Ed. William H. Roberts and Gregoire Turgeon.

    Geneva: Houghton-Mifflin, 1995. 184-86.

King, Martin Luther, Jr. *Where do We Go From Here: Chaos or Community?* Boston: Beacon, 1967.

Post, Elizabeth L. *Emily Post's Etiquette: A Guide to Modern Manners*. 14th ed. New York: Harper, 1984.

Story of English: Pioneers, Oh Pioneers. Videocassette. MacNeil-Lehrer/Gannett Productions/BBC PMI Films,

    1986.

**Process Writing for "Window to the World:
Landscapes Created With the Television and the Automobile"**

Although all major projects in the study of landscape architecture require research, observation, and analysis, most culminate in design drawings rather than the written word. For that reason, I was excited by the research paper assignment given by Terry Clements in my Evolution of the American Landscape course. The paper was to explore the meaning of some aspect or element of the American landscape.

Since the nature of the project required more observation and analysis than library research, my first major task was to choose a topic which I had already begun to explore in my own mind. Actually, deciding on a topic took me longer than writing the paper. Many ideas came to mind, but I needed a subject which I felt I could explore at length without repeating information or running out of valid points. In the end, I chose to examine the combination of two elements: the television and the automobile.

Using two elements allowed me the advantage of two related directions from which to approach my thesis statement. I was surprised at how easily my thoughts came together using both elements. If I had chosen either the television or the automobile alone, it would have been much more difficult to build a supporting framework for the paper's structure.

Within the paper itself, my most difficult task was relating all of my independent thoughts and ideas. I finally chose to divide the paper into sections which explored specific topics interrelated to the whole. I found it easier to follow and make connections this way than with the paper woven together into one continuous exposition.

Writing this paper afforded me the opportunity to organize my thoughts on many issues I have been grappling with throughout my career as a landscape architecture student. I found that the process of bringing these ideas together and explaining them in words provided me with a new level of coherence and understanding in my thinking on these issues.

Janet L. Ford

Window to the World:

Landscapes Created with

the Television and

the Automobile

By

Janet Ford

Evolution of the American Landscape

Professor Terry Clements

11 May 1995

Format

Janet uses headings to separate the sections of her paper. Each documentation style has its own guidelines for how headings should be formatted. Check the stylebook for the documentation system you will be using for formatting requirements.

In this paper, Janet has followed the guidelines for MLA style documentation. There are no specific guidelines for creating subheadings in MLA style. Janet has chosen to use Roman numerals, bold type and capitalized words for her headings.

Titles in academic papers often include a short intriguing phrase followed by a colon that precedes a longer phrase that describes the focus of the paper.

Introduction

The first major section of Janet's paper establishes that the television and the automobile are primary cultural influences in contemporary American life.

Paragraph 1

Janet's thesis paragraph commits her paper to answer the question "How have television the automobile influenced the American man-made landscape and weakened local communities?" It also promises the reader that three particular aspects of the built environment will be examined: the commercial strip, the regional shopping mall, and the suburban residential pattern.

Paragraphs 2-4

Janet places her topic in a historical and cultural context, first providing background on the introduction and development of the automobile, and then moving to the present proliferation of cars in American society. She follows the same pattern in her discussion of television.

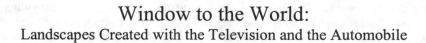

Window to the World:
Landscapes Created with the Television and the Automobile

I. Introduction

Over the past 50 years, the American people have adopted two cultural elements, the television and the automobile, which have been primary influences on their way of seeing and using their communities, their world, and consequently shaping their environment. Together, these two elements have influenced the landscapes of the commercial strip, the regional shopping mall, and the suburban residential pattern. These two products have also induced the demise of boundaries and centers in the man-made landscape, which in turn has caused the weakening of local communities. In combination, the television and the automobile have had profound effects within the built landscape.

At the 1939 World's Fair in New York, visionaries in many emerging technological fields unveiled their ideas of the future. The automobile companies were pushing their magnificent displays of the future of a mobile society in exhibits such as "Highways and Horizons" and "Futurama" by General Motors, "The Amazing Talking Plymouth" by Chrysler, and "The Road of Tomorrow" by Ford. Although the country was deep in depression,

Paragraph 2

Halfway through the paragraph, Janet shifts in time from the 1939 World's Fair to a quotation from a contemporary author writing retrospectively about it. Although the verbs remain in the past tense, thus providing a certain amount of continuity in the prose, the transition could be smoother to aid readers in making the shift from 1939 to Rolfes' 1988 quotation. One possible revision to make the transition more evident would be to give the author's name and book title to introduce the quotation; for example,

> Looking back at the World's Fair, Herbert Rolfes in the book *The World of Tomorrow* comments, "Though no one seemed to notice it at the time,…

Paragraph 3

Janet uses the Modern Language Association (MLA) in-text citation system for documenting her research sources. In MLA style, the author's name and page number typically are given in parentheses immediately after the information taken from the source. If the author's name is used in the body of the sentence, as in Janet's reference to Bennett in paragraph 4, then only the page number is given in the parentheses.

Paragraphs 5-6

Janet notes that the television has replaced the hearth as the new center around which the family gathers in contemporary America. These paragraphs form part of her support for the general idea underlying her paper, that the television is a primary cultural element. She offers brief but convincing evidence for the automobile being another primary influence in paragraph 3 with the statistics she cites.

fairgoers marveled at the fast-paced visions of the luxuries of their future. "And, though no one seemed to notice at the time, the major theme of the most popular attraction of the fair-General Motors' Futurama was that America was going to have to be completely remade in the image of the automobile if it were to reap the benefits of the World of Tomorrow," writes Herbert Rolfes in the book entitled *The World of Tomorrow*. "A vast network of highways was going to change our lives for the better, Bel Geddes (the creator of Futurama) predicted. He was half right" (Zim, Lerner, and Rolfes 97).

Today, approximately 90% of American households own at least one car (Bennett 123). Unthinkable amounts of asphalt draw fast moving lines from city to city, town to town, door to door. The automobile has become a symbol of freedom, opportunity, and convenience.

Another visionary at the fair was the Radio Corporation of America (RCA), which displayed its new form of the radio, which had not only sound, but also pictures. The television was well received, but few people could afford such an expensive price tag during the failing economic times. The Second World War further impeded the launching of the TV into mainstream culture, but this halt was only temporary. By 1951, the war was over, the economy was rejuvenated, and over 10 million American homes contained television sets. By 1970, that figure had jumped to 60 million, or 95% of all U.S. households. In fact, more people own a TV set than have indoor plumbing, points out William J. Bennett in his book *The Index of Leading Cultural Indicators* (103).

"Television became the new family hearth and the new center of American culture," states Steven Lubar in *Infoculture* (242). The hearth has been a traditional element in the theories of architectural origin since Vitruvius, Semper, and Loos spoke of the fire as the beginnings of community. Semper called the hearth the "moral element of architecture" (102). He wrote that it was the element which the floor (the mound), the walls, and the roof were constructed to protect. The hearth was the center of what we may call the family room, today. People gathered around it for warmth, protection, and food. It was the focal point of architecture.

It is striking that the television has been likened to the hearth, "the moral element of architecture" (Semper 102). The TV is indeed the new center of the American family room. According to Bennett,

Paragraph 7
In the concluding paragraph of this section, Janet links her main point to its larger implications.

Photographs
Janet uses a photograph as well as a heading to introduce each major section of her paper. Because her paper focuses on the built landscape, the photos provide not only a pleasing visual element for readers but also strong examples of the types of environments she discusses. Note that MLA style recommends providing a caption for each photo in the paper.

Janet used color photocopying—a perfectly acceptable method—to transfer her original photos into the paper. If you have access to a scanner and photo-manipulation software such as PhotoShop, you can scan the photos onto a disk and then print them out using a laser printer. Doing so allows you to change the resolution, the brightness, and the size of the photos.

in 1992, the average household viewed over seven hours of TV per day (102). Teenagers spent three hours watching TV each day, yet only twenty minutes socializing with their mothers and five minutes with their fathers (103). Bennett also points out that when teens do spend time with their families, it's often spent watching TV (103).

Accepting that television and the automobile have become primary cultural elements which touch nearly every American life on a daily basis, it follows that the values and the way of seeing the world extending from these elements influence the human mind, and thus the environment our collective minds create.

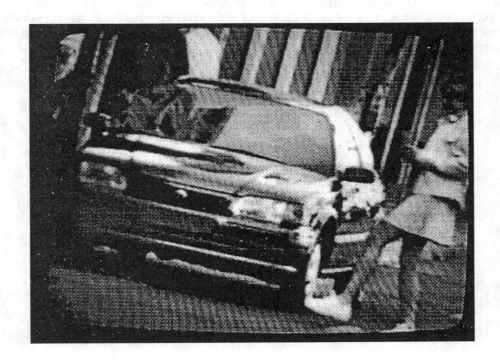

Paragraphs 8-11

Janet establishes the visual techniques used in television in the first paragraph, and in the second creates a metaphor to link these techniques with the visual effects of commercial strips. She supports the metaphor with a quotation from McDonald in the third paragraph. In the next paragraph, Janet ties this connection to a trend in the larger field of architecture.

Janet uses rather short paragraphs throughout her paper. Although a series of short paragraphs can make a paper seem choppy or disorganized, in this paper the brevity of the paragraphs reinforces Janet's points about the contemporary American landscape: its speed, efficiency, and as Janet notes about the mosaic of television, its discontinuities. The format of the paper reflects its content.

II. The Commercial Strip

The commercial strip is one of the most obvious landscapes derived from the influences of the automobile and the television. Television's visual technique is a mosaic of fast-moving thoughts, ideas, and pictures which are juxtaposed, twisted, and turned for quick consumption by the viewer. "For the mosaic is not uniform, continuous, or repetitive," writes Marshall McLuhan in *Understanding Media: Extensions of Man.* "It is discontinuous, skew, and nonlineal, like the actual TV image" (291).

This fragmented nature is reflected in the form of the modern commercial strip. The strip began its most dramatic evolution in the 1950s along with the advent of television. The two elements are intrinsically linked. Traveling along the strip, one is bombarded by hundreds of images, pieces of the landscape strung along the road. The road becomes the length of film, the sign and symbols are the frames, and the movement of the automobile is the method of viewing. Together, it reads much like the moving mosaic of television.

Paragraph 10

It is acceptable in MLA style to provide the complete title and author of the research source within the sentence, as Janet has done in her reference to McDonald's essay. When used repeatedly, however, this style of citation tends to break into the reader's train of thought Several formats are acceptable for MLA-style citations:

- Put the author's name in the sentence, and the page number inside the parentheses.
- Put the title of the source in the sentence, and the author's last name and page number inside the parentheses.
- Put both the author's last name and the page number inside the parentheses.

Varying the way you cite sources allows you to work your citations smoothly into your own prose. Attempt to keep the citations as unobtrusive as possible so that your readers can focus on your major ideas.

Paragraph 12

When Janet quotes Bel Geddes in this paragraph, her parenthetical citation clearly shows readers that she found the quotation in a work written by authors other than Geddes. The abbreviation "qtd. in" ("quoted in") alerts readers that they will find the Works Cited entry for this quotation under the names Zim, Lerner, and Rolfes-not Geddes. This citation also shows the correct style for citing a work by three authors: all three authors' last names are given in the same order in which they appear on the title page of the research source.

Television stresses the importance of visual image above all else for recognition. In his essay "The Commercial Strip: From Main Street to Television Road," Kent McDonald states, "We experience McDonald's, Wendy's, and Exxon, both out on the road and in the transient images of television, and the mutual dependency of the road and television has changed our architecture. The strip has become Television Road" (12).

The billboard architecture of the commercial strip signifies the growing trend towards visual rather than spatial understanding in architecture. Buildings have become signage rather than places. They are viewed as fragmented symbols rather than parts of a whole.

The automobile was expected to facilitate the luxury of speed, which, in turn, would mean convenience. At the 1939 World's Fair, Bel Geddes said, "Today, speed is the cry of our era" (qtd. in Zim, Lerner, and Rolfes 97). It seems things have not slowed down since. Automobiles have changed the concept of distance. Broad distances are quickly covered by the car. The scale of the built environment has grown to reflect this speed. The strip is composed of businesses which once would have crowded the edges of a pedestrian-oriented main street. Today, the landscape surrounding roadways is meant to accommodate cars rather than people. However, the New Urbanism movement in architecture is attempting to harken back to the convenience of dense, walkable neighborhood centers, which reflects a shift from speed as convenience to a place which is not only convenient but experiential.

Television also played a role in the shift towards efficiency and the form of the strip. The time-clock mentality was born with the assembly lines of the industrial revolution and fostered in the regulation of TV land. Stories fit neatly into one-half and one hour packages which conveniently end where the next begins. Today, those shows cycle continuously hour-after-hour, day-after-day, week-after-week. Television thrives on time. Getting the message out quickly and efficiently means big bucks. The strip functions in the same linear regulation with the same goal in mind: profit.

Paragraph 14
Janet introduces the idea of disappearing boundaries and centers in paragraph 1, and she returns to it here as an effect of the automobile's widespread use. Janet assumes correctly that her reader (the instructor of her landscape architecture class) will understand the allusion to the cable car's impact on the garden city concept. She makes a similar assumption about the reader's background knowledge in paragraph 10 when she discusses the trend in architecture toward visual rather than spatial understanding. If Janet were writing for a more general audience, these comments would need to be further explained.

Paragraph 16
Janet writes very generally in this paragraph about changes in the American lifestyle caused by the suburban explosion. In research papers, such assertions should typically be supported by evidence. In this paragraph, such evidence could include a quotation from an expert to back up her statement that "suburbia has become a symbol of the American dream rather than the dream itself." Although Janet may have over-generalized in her description of suburban life, the paragraph is effective in that it provokes very strong visual images in her readers' minds. Visual imagery is one way to make an abstract point more concrete for readers.

III. Suburbia

Efficiency and speed also played a large role in the creation of suburbia. People cherished the ability of their cars to whisk them away from the city and into the country in minutes. People learned they could drive out to the country for a picnic lunch, yet be home by dinner. Soon traditional boundaries disappeared. It didn't take long for developers to see the opportunity for the automobile to continue the garden city concept which the cable car had begun. "Garden cities" began to emerge in the outer fringes of most major cities, and suburban sprawl was born.

Besides reinforcing the notions of efficiency and convenience, TV also played a large role in selling the suburban landscape to millions of Americans. Smiling women in oversized houses fawned over their dishwashing detergents while adorable children played with their new puppies in the sanctity of their own backyards. Suburbia was sold.

The landscape of keeping up with the Joneses meant cookie-cutter houses set back from the street, distanced from neighbors, and miles from downtown. Over time, suburbia has become a symbol of the American dream rather than the dream itself. The yard is now a tiny piece of privatization surrounded by a headache of public infrastructure. Commuters no longer sail through a landscape of open country and fresh air to reach their homes. Instead, they crawl endlessly through miles of gridlock surrounded by the non-descript buffers of the mega-highway

Paragraph 17
This paragraph contains a number of unsupported generalizations, beginning with the third sentence. Research paper writers must carefully lay out their line of evidence in order to convince readers of their reasoning, especially when attempting to show cause-effect relationships. For example, the last sentence needs a variety of evidence—facts, statistics, expert testimony, and the like—to support it completely.

or the fragmented confusion of the commercial strip. In fact, in the average American's attempt to live their above-average dream, most families send both partners out into the work force and the children to day care, leaving no one at home to enjoy their oversized house with its postage stamp-size lawn located at the end of their very private cul-de-sac. What derived from technological efficiency and the dream of uniqueness has become a land of repetition and excess.

IV. The Regional Shopping Mall

Vast technological improvements in recent times have given way to seemingly infinite product varieties, all aimed at the American consumer. Commercials interrupt programming every few minutes to bombard us with product choices. TV itself has moved from information to product. The synoptic views of the world expressed through newscasts, sitcoms, and talk shows are force fed, preprocessed information in a convenient, prepackaged form. Hourly news updates are not intended to inform, but to tantalize, to commercialize, to sell the eleven o'clock news. Television's ability to act as an intrusive salesman has brought about a taste in the American consumer for a wider variety of choices. This craving led to the age of the shopping mall in the 1970s and the 1980s.

Paragraph 17-18

Janet addresses both the television and the automobile, the two main bases of her paper, in relation to the regional shopping mall.

Paragraph 19

The MLA documentation style has a special format for quotations that are longer than four typed lines. The quotation is set off from the left margin one inch. Quotation marks are not used, and the research citation (in this case, "Bl") is placed after the final period of the quotation. The entire quotation is double-spaced.

Television's push for variety and the car's ability to break away from neighborhood limits resulted in the development of the regional shopping mall. The mall became an isolated community based on commercialism. It maintains a privatized, isolated center which is totally internal, surrounded by a sea of parking. Like the strip, the mall is an extension of the television where one recognizes the familiar in an overwhelming flood of choices.

Today, there is evidence that the shopping mall has reached its peak. Catalogs, on-line services, and television shopping networks are offering even more choices with further efficiency and convenience. Shoppers need not venture from their armchairs. Many sites which were planned for future mall construction are now converting those to plans for strip malls because the strip is more convenient to short-term shopping trips. A recent *Washington Post* article written by Margaret Webb Pressler reported:

> A major shift in consumer patterns has left the traditional enclosed mall ... losing ground to newer, more convenient retail development. Consumers, pressed for time and eager for bargains, are turning away in increasing numbers from the marble hallways of enclosed malls, with their department stores and upscale shops. I think this is a temporary solution to the lack of the neighborhood commercial districts which died out with the introduction of the mall. Now that shoppers can make more original purchases through catalogs, TV and the like, they miss the service, convenience, and beauty of the main streets and commercial district which used to be the hearts of their towns.
>
> Instead, they are flocking to decidedly less glamorous strip malls, where shopping is faster and where many of today's hot discount retailers are located. (B1)

The landscape of the regional shopping mall will undoubtedly change again as new uses are found for the massive, isolated complexes. In Pressler's article, Stephen Johnson, the marketing director of Montgomery and Annapolis Malls, suggested that future uses may include community centers and high schools (B3).

Paragraphs 20-26
Janet creates a link between the end of Part 4 and the beginning of Part 5 with the idea of community. However, in moving from the idea of the world as a community to the effects that TV and cars have had on four small communities in Virginia, this section loses some coherence. The statements concerning the four towns are based in Janet's own observations, a valid source of information in a research project. If Janet had been able to locate newspaper articles or editorials that addressed changes in the towns, or interviewed local shopkeepers whose businesses were affected by these changes, readers would be more inclined to accept without reservation the points Janet is making.

V. Main Street

Television has also manipulated and broadened our notion of community. Pictures of people, from distant places speak to us through the TV. The television has become our window to the world. In an instant we are whisked to the middle of custody battles, murder cases, and international wars, in which we have never actually known the participants. Our small town and local communities have been greatly altered by this new view of the world.

The advent of the car as a means of escaping our traditional physical boundaries resulted in suburbia, where there was often no center to begin with, and in the regional shopping mall, which drained the vitality of the main street. The result has left much of our landscape placeless. It is nearly impossible to identify boundaries and centers.

Blacksburg, Christiansburg, Radford, and Salem are four towns in southern Virginia which grew from the building of the railroad. Each town has an identifiable main street that has been drastically affected by the introduction of regional shopping malls. Each main street has been drained of most of its community-oriented shops, and has had to create a new focus for survival.

Paragraph 28
Janet neatly sums up the main argument her paper presents. The conclusion is brief, in keeping with the length of the body of the paper.

Overall Comment
Janet's paper is organized well. She sets up her thesis in the first paragraph and then uses the rest of the introduction to give background information on the television and the automobile. Each major section after the introduction discusses one of the aspects of the built landscape that the television and the automobile have affected. Janet is careful to weave in references to both the television and the automobile in each section.

In any paper that uses several major headings to separate distinct sections, readers are more apt to notice whether the sections each carry approximately the same weight. In Janet's paper, part 3 on "Suburbia" is quite short compared to the sections on the commercial strip and main street. Part 3 includes just three paragraphs and, perhaps more importantly, no research citations. The paper would seem more balanced if each major section included about the same amount of information.

When revising your paper, pay careful attention to the matter of proportion. A lack of balance among your major points can indicate where you need to do more research.

Blacksburg's main street has been the most successful in its reorientation due to a large community of university students who maintain limited access to the automobile. The Blacksburg main street has converted many of its businesses into bars and restaurants that cater to the late-night crowd. Most local residents meet their needs at the regional mall or at Wal-Mart in a strip mall across the street.

Radford is also a university town, but its main street has strived to cater to both the students and the local community. As a result, neither group has its needs filled, and the street is often quiet.

Christiansburg's main street is reminiscent of a ghost town. Although the town is the county's governmental seat, there is little activity downtown except at the courthouse. This main street still seems to be in shock from the desertion of its businesses, but it is slowly leaning towards providing more service-oriented businesses, such as offices and banks, which relate to the governmental seat.

Finally, Salem has also failed to keep the local community interested in its main street. Instead, it is replacing its traditional stores with businesses usually not found in malls, such as craft and antique shops, in an attempt to attract a tourist crowd.

All in all, these local community centers have been forced to appeal to new consumer groups because of the competition of the variety of choices offered by the shopping malls and the bargain prices found along the commercial strip. It is ironic, actually, that the regional shopping center's careless draining of small businesses was, in effect, its own demise. By removing the shops which were convenient to the users, the mall is now being replaced with strip malls which attempt to replace the lost convenience.

VII. Conclusion

Commercial strips, regional shopping malls, and suburban housing patterns are three landscapes which have been greatly influenced by the combination of the television and the automobile. The TV and the car have assured that people are no longer bound by locality. The combination of the TV and automobile has also caused deterioration of the traditional town center. However, the new urbanism movement and the weakening of the regional shopping mall have reflected a trend towards recapturing the convenience, the experience, and the community lost with the death of the town center. In conclusion, over the past forty years, the American landscape has grown rapidly and wildly in response to the television which has shown us the world, and the automobile which has allowed us to get there.

Documentation Format

Janet uses the Modern Language Association (MLA) documentation system. The sources quoted, paraphrased or summarized within the paper are included on a "Works Cited" page. Use the following general rules as a guide in formatting this page:

- Start a new page for "Works Cited."
- Number the page in the same format as the other pages in the paper.
- Center the heading "Works Cited."
- Double-space all lines, and indent the second and subsequent lines of each citation by one half inch.
- Underline or italicize titles of books and periodicals; use quotations marks around titles of articles.
- Alphabetize by main author's last name.
- Sequence the information as follows: author's name, title of article or chapter, title of book or journal, place of publication, publisher, year of publication, and for articles or sections of longer works, the page numbers. Page numbers are not necessary for books.

A typical entry for a "Works Cited" page includes complete publication information for each research source used in the paper. Providing this information allows others who are interested in the topic to locate and read the writer's sources.

In this list, the information given within each entry is complete. The entries for books cite author, title, place of publication, publisher, and date of publication. The entry for the *Washington Post* article provides the author's name, article title, newspaper name, exact date of publication, section letter (B), and page number of the section (1).

The list of "Works Cited" needs to match exactly the references within the body of the paper. For example, the title of Bennett's book as given in paragraph 4 does not match the title given on the Works Cited page. In the text *MacDonald* has a capital *D* while it is not capitalized here. In addition, there is no date for the Semper citation. These types of minor errors, which are very easy to make when noting research sources, need to be eliminated in the editing and proofreading stages of writing a paper.

Fonts and Layout

This manuscript was produced on a home computer in 10-point Times New Roman font, a common choice for research writing. The document is double-spaced, with one-inch margins, and uses the font's italics.

Works Cited

Bennett, William J. *The Index of Leading Cultural Factors*. New York: Touchtone, 1994.

Lubar, Steven. *Infoculture*. Boston: Houghton-Mifflin, 1993.

Macdonald, Kent. "The Commercial Strip: From Main Street to Television Road." *Landscape*. 12-19.

McLuhan, Marshall. *Understanding Media: The Extensions of Man*. New York: Signet, 1964.

Pressler, Mary Webb. "And the Mall Comes Tumbling Down." *The Washington Post*. 9 Nov. 94: B1.

Semper, Gottfried. *The Four Elements of Architecture and Other Writings*. Trans. H.F. Mallgrave.
London: Cambridge UP.

Zim, Larry, Mel Lerner, and Herbert Rolfes. *The World of Tomorrow: The 1939 New York World's Fair*. New York: Harper, 1988.

Process Writing for "Telecommuting: A Case Study"

This was the third of three major projects required for graduation at my school. For this project, students write an in-depth paper on a topic of their own choosing, working one-on-one with a professor over the term.

At first I didn't know what to do. I got the topic of telecommuting from observing my father, who works from home. I wanted to do something original for my paper, and I thought telecommuting might be an interesting topic. When I went to the library, I was surprised to find so much already written about it. Some of the articles were case studies, which suggested a form for my research--I decided to do a case study based on my father.

Originally, I planned to compare the results I got from my own research to the research I found in the library, and to contrast the assertions of the popular press to the findings of the scholarly studies. I thought it would be a fairly easy task to prove or disprove the popular press' hypotheses. At first there seemed to be a clear difference between the popular press and the scholarly research, but the more information I got, the more complex the situation became. The two bodies of research did not always oppose each other in clear ways.

I resolved this problem of approach by deciding not to compare and contrast, but to treat telecommuting as the complex situation it is, and to use my research as an additional, not necessarily opposing, voice.

Originally, too, I was going to do a questionnaire as well as an interview and observation, but once I had done the main interview, I realized that that was all I needed to get the information, though I did call my father a couple of times with follow-up questions.

Organization was the most difficult problem for me. I was worried about repeating information, as well as where to include the new ideas that came to me while I compared the research. The more I wrote, the more ideas I had; but also the more I wrote, the clearer the direction became. Finally, though, it was the deadline that made me decide the paper was finished. (I could keep revising forever.) I got it to a point that I was comfortable with, then turned it in.

James McElroy

Introduction
James begins with a quote that introduces the concept of, but not the term "telecommuting." In the first paragraph James comments on the quote and extends it by incorporating the term and its basic definition.

Paragraphs 2-3
These paragraphs delineate the pros and cons of telecommuting and are important for James' purpose because they establish that the practice of telecommuting has neither a fixed definition nor even a clearly established following.

James is using the Modern Language Association (MLA) footnote system to document his sources. In this system, complete bibliographic information is included at the bottom of the page on which the source is first mentioned. A raised numeral immediately after the reference in the text is keyed to the footnote. Notice that footnotes use a sequence of information that is a bit different from the sequence used on the "Works Cited" page; in a footnote, use the author's first name first, then last name. Follow this with the title of the source; the place, publisher, and year in parentheses; and then the number of the page on which the quote or paraphrase appears.

James McElroy, Jr.

Humanities JOT 5403

Professor John Trimbur

31 March 1992

Telecommuting: A Case Study

Introduction

Today it takes an act of courage to suggest that our biggest factories and office towers may, within our lifetimes, stand half empty, reduced to use as ghostly warehouses or converted into living space. Yet this is precisely what the new mode of production makes possible; a return to cottage industry on a new, higher, electronic basis, and with it new emphasis on the home as the center of society.[1]

Alvin Toffler's view of the future, although extreme even when he expressed it over a decade ago, was not entirely unreasonable. No one today is predicting that entire cities will become ghost towns when people begin to work from their homes. But many believe that modem technology and the changing nature of work are making it increasingly desirable for large segments of the population to work at home through telecommuting, the process of substituting telecommunication for physical commuting.

Articles in the popular media and in trade journals have enthusiastically extolled the virtues of this new "mode of production." A headline in an office technology magazine recently described telecommuting as "A Feeling of Euphoria."[2] A writer for a regional magazine in California went even further, claiming that with telecommuting,

[1] Alvin Toffler, The Third Wave (New York: William Morrow, 1980) 210.

[2] Lee Teschler, "Business Technologies," Modern Office Technology and Industry Week Supplement Sept. 1991: 1.

Although the footnote system is not as frequently used as the in-text citation style, it can be useful if you want your readers to identify quickly the sources you have used. In his paper, James refers to many sources in the first few pages; footnotes let his readers quickly check the sources without having to flip continually to the "Works Cited" page.

Paragraph 4
In this paragraph James tries to find the area of overlap and agreement among the views on telecommuting. He needs to do this in order to show to the reader that telecommuting is indeed a topic worthy of further research. The statistic in the last sentence helps to strengthen this notion.

Paragraph 5
James further strengthens his assertion that telecommuting is worth studying by listing the well-known corporations currently using or researching telecommuting.

In paragraph 5 James includes information from three sources, but only needs to use one footnote since the information is handled as one idea in the paragraph. Separate multiple sources with a semicolon.

". . . the winner is ... . . . the winner is ...everyone ... The city as an employer wins ... The city as an environment wins ... Telecommuters win ... Even telemanagers win ... Some even claim it's like being born again!"[3]

Other articles, and much of the research on telecommuting, have been decidedly more reserved. A contributor to Management World stated that "Dramatic advances in office technology, which may seem to offer exceptional lifestyle conveniences, can represent a minefield."[4] Margrethe Olson, a professor at NYU who has written many articles on the subject, concluded that, "Based on existing research, we cannot predict that telework [telecommuting],[5] as defined and practiced today, will become a prevalent form of work organization-in the future."[6]

Yet actual statistics indicate that telecommuting is practiced by an increasingly significant portion of the work force. Statistics on telecommuting are difficult to compare since there is not a single widespread definition of the telecommuter; while some researchers use the term to include workers who operate their own businesses out of their homes, others define telecommuters as workers who bring extra work home with them from the office at night. Nonetheless, numerous recent sources seem to agree that by the beginning of 1992 there were approximately five to six million telecommuters working full-time from their homes in the United States.

Furthermore, a variety of corporations and government agencies have experimented with telecommuting, including GTE, Travelers Insurance, AT&T in coordination with the state of Arizona, the Washington State Energy

[3] Jack M. Nilles, "How to Plan For and Supervise Telecommuters," Western City Feb. 1991: 3.

[4] James E. Challenger, "Telecommuters Risk Becoming Invisible Workers," Management World W 1992: 8.

[5] Margrethe H. Olson uses the terms telework and telecommuting interchangeably in "Organizational Barriers to Professional Telework," in Homework, ed. Eileen Boris and Cynthia Daniels (Urbana: U of Chicago, 1989) 216.

[6] Olson 226.

Paragraph 6

This is James' purpose statement and rationale for using a case study.

Paragraph 7

James introduces the subject of the case study. He keeps this introduction concise, giving only enough details to orient the reader about McElroy's work.

Paragraph 8 - 22

James uses the structural pattern he established in the introduction (definition - pros - cons) to give readers a familiar sense of direction in this section.

Office, the state of California, Pacific Bell, Bell Atlantic, Illinois Bell, J.C. Penny, Apple Computer, and most recently, the Federal government.[7]

Clearly, even though telecommuting appears to be a growing phenomenon, the issues, problems, and benefits associated with it are still not fully understood. The purpose of this paper is to examine telecommuting from the perspective of a single telecommuter through the use of a case study. It is hoped that the level of detail made possible by a case study will give a fuller understanding of the sometimes conflicting findings cited in research and popular literature.

Jim McElroy, Sr., the subject of the case study, was chosen because of his extensive experience with telecommuting under a variety of different circumstances. He received a masters degree in mechanical engineering from Northeastern University in 1972 and presently is the Eastern U.S. and European business manager for MicroModule Systems of Cupertino, California, "the largest fully merchant manufacturer of multichip modules in the industry today," according to a company brochure. Data was gathered from the case study through a full day interview and observation period. A list of the questions that were used as the basis of the interview can be found in Appendix 1.

Definition of Telecommuter

Since the term has been applied to entirely different groups of workers by different researchers, a precise definition of the term is necessary before comparing research on the subject. According to Jack Nilles, who is credited with originating the term,[8] telecommuting is "the physical decentralization of work by

---

[7] Shari Caudron, "Working at Home Pays Off," Personnel Journal Nov. 1992: 40; Dori Sera Bailey and Jill Foley, "Pacific Bell Works Long Distance," HRMagazine Aug. 1990: 50; Teschler 1; Julian Weiss, "Commuting at the Crossroads," The World & I Dec. 1992: 83.

[8] See margin note in Nilles 3.

Paragraphs 8 - 9
James restates the definition of telecommuting, using the definition written by Jack Nilles. Since Nilles coined the term, his definition adds weight to James' paper.

Paragraph 9
What "neither" refers to is rather unclear, but it is obvious that James wants to stress that there are many forms of telecommuting besides working from the home.

Paragraphs 10 - 16
These paragraphs, which present the popular press' view, constitute the "pros" of Telecommuting.

moving the work to the workers instead of moving the workers to the work."[9] He considers it to be a form of telework, which is "any form of work-related substitution of telecommunications for travel. Such as picking up the phone to talk to someone instead of making the trip to see him/her."[10]

Neither of these terms limit such work to the home office. Telecommuting can alternatively take place from a satellite office, "a relatively self-contained organizational division that is physically located away from the central office,"[11] or from a neighborhood office, created when "the performance of most or all of the central office functions are performed at several regional locations."[12] Employees might work with other people from their company at a neighborhood office, but they don't necessarily work with people from their group there. Although satellite offices are common today (as in the case of a branch of a bank),[13] neighborhood offices remain largely a future possibility.

Popular Press Versus Research Literature

While neither the popular press nor the research literature is unanimous in its respective findings on telecommuting, there are enough similarities within each group to make useful a comparison between the two. In the following section, reports from companies that have experimented with telecommuting are included with the popular press, since both groups tend to base their findings on non-scientific surveys of employees and provide little or no empirical data to back up their findings.

[9]Nilles 3.

[10]Nilles 3.

[11]Reagan Mays Ramsower, Telecommuting: The Organizational and Behavioral Effects of Working At Home (Ann Arbor: UMI Research, 1985) 19.

[12]Ramsower 20.

[13]Ramsower 22.

Paragraph 11
Before going on to give specifics, James summarizes the view of the popular press.

Paragraph 12
James begins to provide specific details to illustrate the popular press view. The statistics are both interestingly informative and effective in allowing James to raise the central issue of telecommuting, the issue of productivity.

The popular press generally cites two primary benefits of telecommuting: increased productivity and greater work satisfaction. The latter is typically attributed to telecommuters having greater freedom and flexibility in their work day. This factor, in addition to telecommuters facing fewer interruptions at home than at the office, is thought to explain the productivity increase.

While it is hard to measure worker satisfaction, many sources cite numbers supporting the increased productivity. Pacific Bell found through a survey of managers that 64% thought telecommuting could increase productivity.[14] Control Data employees who telecommuted claimed productivity increases ranging from 5-100%, with an average increase of 35%.[15] Managers at Bell Atlantic reported increases of up to 200%.[16] Summarizing the overall findings of corporate telecommuting experiments to date, Jack Nilles claimed "the average telecommuter effectiveness typically increases 15% or more in their supervisor's estimation, if both supervisor and telecommuter are properly trained."[17]

Although receiving less emphasis than worker satisfaction and productivity, other benefits are often reported by popular media, including the ability to employ previously unemployable workers (mainly the handicapped), reduced employee turnover and absenteeism, and reduced costs for the employer. An article in Western City reported that the state of California realized a savings of $990,000 for the 150 people in its telecommuting pilot project.[18]

[14]Bailer and Foley 51.

[15]Ronald A. Manning, "Control Data Corporation: Alternate Work Site Programs," in Office Workstations in the Home, by the Board on Telecommunications and Computer Applications, the Commission on Engineering and Technical Systems, and the National Research Council (Washington, D.C.: National Academy) 45.

[16]Weiss 85.

[17]Nilles 4.

[18]Nilles 5.

Paragraph 14
James shows that the popular press view is not completely optimistic. Always taking care to balance the pros and the cons of the situation gives James' paper a tone of thoughtful rationality.

Paragraph 16
James reemphasizes the popular press' main contention that problems with telecommuting are easily solved. This sets up the transition to the researchers' view since it is the point that researchers primarily dispute.

Paragraph 17
This transitional paragraph signals to readers that James will now present the "cons" of telecommuting. Notice how it picks up the idea of simple solutions from the previous paragraph.

Costs also represent one of the drawbacks cited by the popular media, however. In some cases, part of the savings realized by an employer is due to increased costs for the employee. Telecommuting necessitates using the home phone for business calls, an expense that sometimes is not picked up by the employer. In addition, some telecommuters are responsible for purchasing their own office equipment. Overall, though, the popular media view most of the problems commonly associated with telecommuting as being obstacles that can be overcome, not as fundamental flaws with the system.

For example, one problem with telecommuting is convincing managers to trust employees they can not see: "There's still plenty of people who think, 'if I can't see 'em working, they're not working.' "[19] The media point out that this obstacle can be overcome by good management, emphasizing that the growing trend in management for all workers (not just telecommuters) is towards management by objective, not by supervision: "There is no magic here. Effective telemanagement is simply effective management. The difference is that in the office you can say you're managing by objectives ... but telemanagers must do it that way."[20]

By simply following sound policies, then, the popular media emphasizes that telecommuting can provide employees and employers with tangible and significant benefits and with few drawbacks. Furthermore, if problems do come up, they are easily overcome: "Where the results are below expectations, find out why. Most can be fixed. Make the necessary changes. Keep going through this process until telecommuting seems to be just business as usual."[21]

While supporting some of the claims made by the popular press, most research-oriented publications claim that telecommuting results in serious problems for both the employee and the employer, many of which have no simple solutions.

[19]Weiss 85.

[20]Nilles 6.

[21]Nilles 7.

Paragraph 18
James describes the first of three problems of telecommuting. He begins the paragraph with the word, "one," which signals to the readers that it is part of a list.

Paragraph 19
The words "A more serious problem" signal the second problem, that of career advancement. Direct quotes from two sources add weight to the seriousness of the problem.

One such problem is that telecommuters lose face-to-face contact with coworkers that can not necessarily be replaced by other means of communication: "Telecommunications technologies can provide substitutes for face-to-face interactions, but the extent to which these substitutes provide satisfaction levels comparable to those supplied by face-to-face interactions remains largely unexplored."[22] Perhaps because of this lack of face-to-face communication, another researcher found that telecommuting reduces the level of interaction between employees.[23]

A more serious problem cited by researchers is that telecommuting can threaten a worker's advancement in the company. Several researchers commented that workers who are not in the office tend to become invisible and therefore suffer reduced chances of promotion. Reagan Ramsower, the author of one of the most comprehensive studies on telecommuting to date, wrote, "as a telecommuter, their job will offer little hope for advancement. . ."[24] A management trade magazine agreed, warning:

> Employers do not usually take into their confidence people they rarely see, and usually don't view them in the same light as workers they see every day. The individual can become as indispensable as an on-call consultant who is not considered a co-worker, but a resource. The loss of visibility impacts greatly on personal advancement.[25]

[22] Arthur P. Brief, "Effects of Work Location on Motivation," in <u>Office Workstations in the Home</u> 66.

[23] Olson 224.

[24] Ramsower 85.

[25] Challenger 8.

Paragraphs 20 - 21
"Furthermore" signals the third and most serious problem, productivity. James could have used the signal words "first," "second," and "third," but chose to use a subtler method.

These paragraphs provide a contrast to paragraph 12, in which James shows the extreme optimism of the popular press. Devoting two paragraphs to the problem, as well as citing researchers' findings, helps him to persuade readers that the problems are complex.

Paragraph 22
James ends with a note of seriousness. He does not want to try to resolve the problems or to argue one way or the other. His purpose is to add to our knowledge of telecommuting, not to present any hard and fast answers.

Furthermore, researchers question the benefits cited in popular sources, especially the increase in productivity claimed by many telecommuters. In a preview to a collection of corporate literature on telecommuting, Ramsower commented:

It should be noted that the results and conclusions stated in the following discussion are based upon very limited and often subjective information taken from the popular literature. The author could not find a single case in which an empirical organizational experiment of telecommuting was undertaken and publicly reported. Therefore, this discussion should be viewed as one that espouses the currently-held beliefs about telecommuting, which are largely without substantiation.[26]

Even if the increased productivity claims can be substantiated, though, some researchers believe that telecommuters get more done simply because they work longer hours. Since productivity is often measured in terms of the standard eight-hour work day, not in terms of the actual time spent working, this is a real possibility. A popular source verified "several participants worked regularly beyond the normal eight hours a day because it was convenient and easy to do at home." [27] Ramsower added, "There is little evidence in this study to suggest that full-time telecommuting can increase productivity by increasing performance. Productivity can only be increased for full-time telecommuters by decreasing their labor costs."[28]

The overall impression of telecommuting given by research is that it is far from the euphoria that the popular literature portrays it as, particularly in the case of full-time telecommuting. Ramsower concluded,

[26]Ramsower 12.

[27]Nelson Phelps, "Mountain Bell: Program for Managers," in <u>Office Workstations in the Home</u> 36.

[28]Ramsower 90.

Paragraph 23 – 25
James uses narrative to present the background for his case study. The story creates interest in Jim, and allows James to succinctly give the necessary background information.

"Full-time telecommuting produced many negative organizational and behavioral effects," and added, "Generally, these results do not support the contention that full-time telecommuting is likely to become a widespread work alternative."[29]

Case Study Background

Jim's experience with telecommuting began in 1985 when he was managing a design group at Digital Equipment Corporation. While at Digital he telecommuted part-time solely to supplement the time he spent in his office (which was located about 45 minutes from his New Hampshire home). Digital had no official telecommuting program at the time. The company simply let individual managers decide whether telecommuting was right for their employees. Jim explained that his boss utilized telecommuting primarily to get more work from his employees: "He figured the longer you worked, the more you got done."

Although Digital had no official telecommuting program, it loaned telecommuting employees a computer terminal and a modem at no charge, and it paid the phone costs associated with using the modem. This equipment enabled Jim to access his electronic mail (email) from home, and the time he spent working at home was primarily devoted to reading and replying to email messages, of which he received about 100 a day. He explained that since he was often at meetings during much of the day, the time he spent at the terminal in the evening was often the only time he could catch up on his email.

In 1989, the group Jim worked for was transferred to California. He moved with them and became a manufacturing engineer in charge of 500 people. While living in California, he continued to telecommute part-time from home to read email. He never planned on living in California permanently, though, and after spending three years there he moved back to New Hampshire, even though doing so required him to give up his old management position. Since all of his coworkers were still in California, the only way Jim could continue working with them while living on the East Coast was by full-time telecommuting. He arranged to work from a Digital building in

[29]Ramsower 92.

Paragraph 26
Within the narrative of Jim's career James inserts this paragraph describing the telecommuting policies of the companies for which Jim has worked.

Paragraphs 27-28
James continues the narrative of Jim's use of telecommuting.

Paragraph 29
James inserts information from the research ("Much of the current research). This allows him to show the connections between the research and his own study. By presenting his study within the context of scholarly research, he imparts a scholarly tone to his paper.

Nashua, New Hampshire, essentially using it as a neighborhood office, and took on the position of sales manager (which did not involve any management responsibilities). After the California group separated from Digital to become MicroModule Systems (MMS) in June of 1992, Jim moved out of the Digital office and began telecommuting full-time from home.

Jim is the only MMS employee who works from his home; while other employees telecommute part-time in much the same manner Jim used to, they all spend their days at MMS' headquarters in Cupertino, California. As was the case with Digital, MMS has no official telecommuting program, but it does provide employees with computers for home use.

Jim's current job title is "Eastern U.S. & European Business Manager," the same position he took when he first returned to New Hampshire. Although he would have preferred to keep his old management position, he said it would have simply been impossible to manage 500 people from across the country. Some research on telecommuting has suggested remote management is possible under certain circumstances, but because Jim had no experience with it, the issue was not examined in this paper.

Jim's primary responsibilities are in sales, marketing, and applications engineering, which he defined as "helping a customer figure out what technology is best for a given application." In carrying out these responsibilities, Jim works with three distinct groups of people: his coworkers at MMS (primarily other employees of the marketing division), representatives (people hired by MMS to promote its products to potential buyers), and customers themselves.

Case Study Findings

Jim's telecommuting experiences are unique in that he has had experience with three distinct forms of telecommuting: part-time from home, full-time from a neighborhood office, and full-time from home. Much of the current research on telecommuting identifies such distinctions as being important to the outcome of telecommuting. In Jim's case, however, direct comparisons between full-time telecommuting and part-time telecommuting are impossible because the nature of Jim's job was different in each case. Furthermore, Jim identified few

Paragraph 31

Again, James incorporates researchers' findings. He also presents the specifics of Jim's work situation and describes the problems that annoy him. Though these are real problems, they are not the problems cited by James as being central to telecommuting (face-to-face communication, career advancement, and productivity). He could strengthen this paragraph by mentioning how this information about office equipment and the phone illustrates the researcher's findings.

Paragraph 32

Jim does provide this link to the major problems associated with telecommuting in this paragraph. He begins with the first of the three problems--face-to-face communication—that he mentioned earlier (in paragraph 18).

differences between working at home and working at a neighborhood office. Therefore, the findings that follow apply to his experience both at the neighborhood office and at home, except where noted.

MicroModule Systems has equipped Jim's office with several pieces of telecommunications equipment, giving him a wide variety of mediums over which he can contact his coworkers, representatives, and customers. This equipment includes a facsimile machine, a copier, and a personal computer equipped with a modem and an ink jet printer. Since Jim relies heavily on the phone, MMS installed two additional phone lines in his home office (one for fax and modem use and one for a traditional phone). It also provided him with an answering machine.

Most researchers argue that modern technology makes it possible to duplicate the equipment of the office in the home, and in most cases Jim agreed. Although less expensive and not as advanced as the equipment in the office, his fax, copier, and computer are sufficient for the tasks he uses them for. The one exception was his present phone system. He explained that his primitive answering machine (which is almost ten years old) was simply no match for the voice mail system he used at the office (both in Nashua and in California). In addition to being more-versatile in its message handling capabilities (voice mail lets users forward calls to other people within the office), voice mail also has the ability to take a message while someone is on the phone. Since his home office phone does not have this ability, Jim's coworkers insisted he get call waiting so that they could get through when he is on the phone. While this makes it easier for them to reach Jim, his phone conversations are sometimes interrupted two or three times per call by incoming calls. "It's a pain in the neck," he said.

Some of the technology that is available, however, is simply too expensive f or Jim to use. Teleconferencing, for example, promises to provide a better substitute for face-to-face conversations than present means of communication. But its cost is exorbitant, and Jim noted that even when he worked in an office, video conferences were rare. Telephone conferences, on the other hand, are utilized by Jim daily. While a telephone conference is no different than a traditional phone call in that both use the same piece of equipment, Jim distinguished phone conferences as being planned phone calls, similar in some respects to a meeting.

Paragraphs 33-35
James drops his direct discussion of the problem of face-to-face communication, but addresses it indirectly by describing Jim's office equipment and how he uses it to communicate with fellow employees.

Paragraph 35
James goes on to describe Jim's rationale for using the telecommunication media available to him. (Not included here)

Paragraphs 36-37
James returns to a key researcher, Reagan Ramsower, to begin his next and very important section. He summarizes this researcher's findings in order to set his own study against them.

Although Jim uses the phone for much of his communication needs, he estimated that he spends just as much time using email. Unlike his home phone system, the equipment he uses for email at home is no different from the equipment he used at the office. In fact, his computer was actually taken from a vacant office at MMS in California.

While using email accounts for most of the time Jim spends on his computer, he also uses it for another form of communication, albeit an untraditional one: spreadsheets. While spreadsheets might not be considered communication in the normal sense,[30] they enable Jim to send and receive complicated sales data to coworkers in California. Ironically, the company's present computer network makes it necessary for him to send these files physically by disk instead of electronically.

Not all of his communication is carried out electronically, however. Jim still sends hard copies of documents to the office at times. He also makes use of express mailing services; he estimated that Federal Express stops by his house at least once a week.

Effects of Telecommuting on Communication

Reagan Ramsower reached a number of interesting conclusions regarding the effect telecommuting has on communications.[31] He found that telecommuters communicate less with workers of all levels (superiors, subordinates, and coworkers) and that the communicating a telecommuter does consists primarily of asking questions related to a current problem. Furthermore, such communication was found to be strictly work-related and of an informational nature; conversational communication simply ceased to exist: "Full-time telecommuters discard any communication needs that are not of this [informational] type."[32]

---

[30]Dorothy A. Winsor, "What Counts as Writing? An Argument from Engineer's Practice," College Composition and Communication 41 (1990): 58.

[31]Ramsower 59.

[32]Ramsower 73.

Paragraph 38
In this transition paragraph between the summary of Ramsower and his own study, saying that he does not totally disagree with Ramsower makes both James and Jim appear moderate and rational.

Paragraph 39
This paragraph presents Jim's (and, therefore, James') basic agreement with the research.

Paragraphs 40 - 41
This presents Jim's (and James') basic disagreement with the research.

Paragraph 42
In the first sentence James refers to the claims of "some research," but has neglected to document the source. Documentation is necessary here since he includes the source's material.

Ramsower also found that although telecommuters substitute the phone for face-to-face conversation for asking questions, this does not affect the time periods during which they can get questions answered. Finally, Ramsower found that full-time telecommuters have a need for face-to-face communication: "While it was evident that the telephone moderated their decreased communication, the technology was unable to fully substitute for all communications." The telephone is, however, "an adequate media for asking questions and talking to others."[33]

Jim's experiences supported some of Ramsower's findings, but in many cases he disagreed, either wholly or in part, to the conclusions reached by Ramsower.

Jim was unable to determine whether he faced reduced levels of communication while working at home because his job in the traditional office was different from his present one. He did find that he now uses the phone to a much greater extent than he did when at the office, and he estimated that he spends as much time on the computer using email.

Contrary to the research findings, Jim uses the phone (and email) for much more than simply asking questions about current problems. Furthermore, he finds that he still has conversational phone calls at home, although "there is less of that." He stated that there is more time for casual conversation when one is face-to-face with someone.

Jim's experience also directly contradicted another research finding: that telecommuters found relying on the phone to ask questions does not reduce the times when they can get the questions answered. When he was in the office himself, he could track people down if he needed to, a task that is difficult over the phone. Jim also disagreed with the conclusion that the phone is adequate for asking questions. Many questions, he explained, are best answered using diagrams and sketches, which requires using a fax in addition to the traditional phone.

Although not one of Ramsower's conclusions, some research speculated that telecommuters might increase their communications simply because they are easier to reach at home, where they will not be pulled away from their office by a meeting or other distraction. Telecommuters (including Jim) often use cordless phones when working at home so that even if they do have to step out of the "office," they still can be reached. In Jim's experience, he found that it was easier for people to get in touch with him at home. In fact, this was a problem in

[33]Ramsower 74.

Paragraph 43

The main problem-productivity-is now addressed, linking to paragraphs 12, 20 and 21. Since James has earlier presented productivity as a major problem, he could have discussed it in greater depth here.

James goes on to discuss the differences between working at the office and telecommuting. (Not included here)

Paragraph 45

James explains how his case study adds to what we know about telecommuting, and how his study reveals the shortcomings of previous research.

some cases; forced to use call waiting, Jim finds that many important conversations are interrupted by other calls. However, when he is on the road, Jim said that it becomes much more difficult for people to reach him. When he was a full-time office worker, an inter-office phone mail system made it easier for him to retrieve calls even when he was on the road. The answering machine he uses now requires a beeper to retrieve messages remotely, a device Jim finds so annoying that he never uses it. Instead, he calls home several times during the day and has his wife repeat any messages that are left on the machine.

When asked about his productivity, Jim replied that usually he finds his work at home to be more efficient than his work at the office. "Where it hurts you, though, is that you don't have all the support services at home." Although much of the research found that technology has made it possible to duplicate the functions of office machinery and electronics, Jim found that in some cases there still were not viable alternatives. There is no way for telecommuters to have access to their own secretary or copy center at home. While telecommuters themselves carry out many of the tasks traditionally provided for them at the office, doing so requires spending extra time and therefore possibly mitigates any productivity increases.

Conclusions and Suggestions

As is true for any case study, the observations cited in this paper can not by themselves prove or disprove existing research. What they can do, however, is suggest areas where new research may be useful, in addition to pointing to deficiencies in present research.

While Jim's experiences with telecommuting support to some extent the research done to date, his explanations as to how and why he chooses to use certain mediums of communication reveal that most of the present research has not fully grasped the complexities behind such decisions. Jim often accepts the limitations imposed by certain mediums in return for advantages they offer over mediums researchers traditionally identify as ideal.

Paragraph 46
Continuing with the ideas in paragraph 45, James suggests topics for further studies. Paragraphs 45 and 46 include what researchers commonly include at the end of their papers: encouragement to other researchers to continue the search for knowledge about the subject matter.

Overall Comment
James' paper shows a thoroughness of research that makes his paper scholarly and convincing. The quantity of his interview questions helped him to gather a wealth of detailed responses that he then used either to support or to question the research. If James had only done the interview and observation, with little or no library research, he may have been able to make the same comments, but they would certainly not have been very convincing. His case study is useful because it is set within the context of more broadly focused or comprehensive research.

By including the research by the popular press, James is able to broaden the context. The popular press' optimistic findings make a useful contrast to the more scholarly studies. James can treat his own findings as yet another voice in the debate, rather than setting himself in opposition to just one set of findings.

Furthermore, Jim's experiences with a neighborhood office as compared to his home office illustrate some of the factors behind increased productivity that are not cited in research. While new technology does allow professionals to assume tasks that used to be handed down to secretaries (typing, copying, etc.), doing so requires extra time on the part of the professional. It might be worthwhile to examine whether the increased flexibility afforded to telecommuters is cost effective; after all, it does not make sense to pay a top executive hundreds of dollars an hour to use a copier when a secretary can do the same task for substantially less.

In any case, it is clear that although telecommuting might be becoming commonplace, a great deal more research remains to be done if this new "mode of production" is to be fully understood.

Appendix

Use the heading "Appendix" and center it on the page; use a separate page for each appendix. The format of the appendix is flexible, determined by the material that you are including in it. Choose a format that presents the material in a clearly understandable way. You may need to use captions for maps, tables, charts, and other visuals, or you may need to provide headings. For instance, James has labeled this appendix, "Interview Questions," and has provided subheads for the categories of questions he asked.

Interview Questions

As you can see, James has questions that will help him gather a wealth of details. Even though most of his questions are yes/no and objective-answer questions, it is clear from the paper that James has followed those questions with a "why," "how," or "what is your opinion on that" prompt.

Appendix 1

Interview Questions

History of working at home:

1. Does or did Digital have a formal work-at-home program?
2. When did you first start bringing work home with you?
3. What was the nature of this work?
4. How much time did you normally spend doing this work? If unable to give a specific value, what was the range of time you might have spent at home?
5. What equipment did you use for this work?
6. How exactly did you use this equipment?
7. Did you communicate with other office workers while you were at home?
8. If so, were these other workers at home also or were they still at the office?
9. Why did you start working at home?
10. What differences did you see in the work you did at home as opposed to the work you did at the office?
11. Were you more productive at home?
12. Did you save certain work for home?
13. Did working at home affect the work you did in the office?
14. What limitations did you see with working from home?
15. Did you use email at the office for the same purposes as email at home?

Background on present situation:

1. How long have you been working full-time at home?
2. Whose idea was it to work at home?
3. How have others felt about this?
4. Do other employees at MMS work at home?
5. If so, do they work full-time at home?
6. What are some of your general impressions about working at home?
7. How would your work be different if you still worked in the office?
8. How long have you been using email? How did you learn to use email? How did you learn the other software you presently use?
9. What are your actual day-to-day job tasks?
10. Do you supervise anyone?
11. Do you still have an office in California?

Methods and choices of communication:

1. How much time do you estimate you spend: on the phone? reading email? writing email? using other forms of communication?
2. Do you feel the communications you have with the office and others is adequate?
3. How do you decide on which medium to use? Is this influenced by who you are communicating with?

84

1. What are your impressions of each communication medium?
2. How does your use of communications equipment differ from when you worked in an office?
3. Specifically, do you use certain means of communication for different purposes than when you worked at the office?
4. How do you cope with not being able to attend meetings?
5. How does not being able to meet with people face-to-face affect your work?
6. Did you have an internal voice mail system at your previous location? Did you use its advanced features? Does not having a system with similar abilities affect your present work?
7. Are your other home communication products similar to those you used at work?
8. How do you communicate with your manager?
9. How are you kept apprised of company policies and such? How were you kept apprised of this information when you worked at the office?
10. Do you feel you miss out on information that is traded throughout the office in casual conversation?
11. When communicating with someone in a social manner, what medium of communication do you use? Has this affected the time you spend in such communication?
12. How do you ask questions of others (using what communications)?
13. What do you talk about on the phone?

Face-to-face communication:

1. Do you feel more comfortable either on the phone or when talking face-to-face?
2. Do you feel comfortable in general in a sales position?
3. What do you substitute for face-to-face conversations?
4. Are you involved with deal-making?
5. How do you decide when to travel?

Interaction with boss:

1. Does your boss supervise and evaluate you and your work?
2. Do you feel working at home has affected your chances of promotion? How would you describe your relationship with your boss (i.e. adversaries, partners, etc.)?
3. How has working at home made you more or less independent of your boss?
4. Has the amount of work you're responsible for changed since you started working at home?
5. What kinds of things do you discuss with your boss?

Documentation Format

James uses the Modern Language Association (MLA) footnote documentation system. The sources quoted, paraphrased or summarized within the paper are included on a "Works Cited" page. Use the following general rules as a guide in formatting this page:

- Start a new page for "Works Cited."
- Number the page in the same format as the other pages in the paper.
- Center the heading "Works Cited."
- Double-space all lines, and indent the second and subsequent lines of each citation by one half inch.
- Underline titles of books and periodicals; use quotations marks around titles of articles.
- Alphabetize by main author's last name.
- Sequence the information as follows: author's name, title of article or chapter, title of book or journal, place of publication, publisher, year of publication, and for articles or sections of longer works, the page numbers. Page numbers are not necessary for books.

Note that the sequence of information is different from the sequence in the footnotes. The alphabetizing by author's last name helps readers quickly find a particular researcher.

Font and Layout

This work is produced by McElroy in 10-point Times New Roman a common font and one well-suited to this type of manuscript. This computer-produced document is double-spaced, with one-inch margins and type is flush left, ragged right.

Works Cited

Bailey, Dora Sera, and Jill Foley. "Pacific Bell Works Long Distance." HRMagazine Aug. 1990: 50.

Board of Telecommunications and Computer Applications, Commission on Engineering and Technical Systems,

    and National Research Council, eds. Office Workstations in the Home. Washington, D.C.: National

    Academy, 1985.

Brief, Arthur P. "Effects of Work Location on Motivation." Board of Telecommunications and Computer

    Applications, Commission on Engineering and Technical Systems, and National Research Council.

Caudron, Shari. "Working at Home Pays Off." Personnel Journal Nov. 1992: 40.

Challenger, James E. "Telecommuters Risk Becoming Invisible Workers." MW Winter 1992: 8.

Manning, Ronald A. "Control Data Corporation: Alternative Work Site Programs." Board of Telecommunications

    and Computer Applications, Commission on Engineering and Technical Systems, and National Research

    Council.

Nilles, Jack M. "How to Plan for and Supervise Telecommuters." Western City Feb. 1991: 3.

Olson, Margrethe H. "Organization Barriers to Professional Telework." Homework, eds. Eileen Boris and Cynthia
    R. Daniels. Urbana: U of Illinois P, 1989. 215-30.

Phelps, Nelson. "Mountain Bell: Program for Managers." Board of Telecommunications and Computer

    Applications, Commission on Engineering and Technical Systems, and National Research Council.

Ramsower, Reagan Mays. Telecommuting: The Organizational and Behavioral Effect of Staying at Home.

    Ann Arbor: UMI Research Press, 1985.

Teschler, Lee. "Business Technologies." Modern Office Technology and Business Week Sept. 1991: 1BT.

Toffier, Alvin. The Third Wave. New York: William Morrow, 1980.

Weiss, Julian. "Telecommuting at the Crossroads." The World & I Dec. 1992: 82.

Winsor, Dorothy A. "Engineering Writing/Writing Engineering." College Composition and Communication

    41 (Feb. 1990): 58.

Introduction to Nonlinear Research Presentations

In the past, undergraduate research was carried out mainly in a library where carefully handwritten notes were made on index cards and papers were painstakingly typed on a manual typewriter . They were then handed directly to a professor, who was likely to be the only reader of the work. Since the early 1990's, however, technology has affected every aspect of the research assignment. You may find yourself operating differently than students in the past did. The old drawers containing index cards have given way to online card catalogs. Printed periodical indexes have been supplemented by rapidly updated CD-ROM indexes that often contain full text articles as well as citations for materials in hundreds of periodicals. The World Wide Web has made vast numbers of files that originate in every part of the world available with the click of a mouse as you sit before your home computer. Papers are now keyboarded using word processing software and enriched with graphics, audio and video by way of multimedia software and shareware that can be downloaded from the Internet. You can even build links within the sections of the paper as well as with other Internet sites. Finally you can publish your papers on the web for all the world to read.

Most libraries have now added CD-ROM resources to their traditional collections. A single disk can contain entire encyclopedias or large archival collections of primary source materials. In addition, libraries subscribe to CD-ROM databases of periodical reference materials. Contents of CD-ROMs vary, but may include indexes of citations for print materials, abstracts, full-text articles, audio and video clips as well as graphics and photographs that are all linked to one another.

Another electronic source of information is the World Wide Web (WWW), a multimedia portion of the Internet that links millions of files together. By a simple point and click approach, you can search for very specific topics all the way up to very broad subjects that yield lists of millions of files. These files vary in nature and may include text, graphical, sound and/or video clips, which can be downloaded to your computer and modified or printed as seen. Much that is on the web is undocumented and you'll quickly see why you must carefully identify the sources you choose to use for your project. New formats have been developed for citing electronic resources such as the Columbia Online Citation Guidelines, so you'll want to be sure your research style guide is current.

To access the Web, you simply log onto a computer connected to the Internet by using a communications program called a Web browser. A browser automates the process of requesting information from other computers and displays this information in a formatted structure on the computer screen. Today, the World Wide Web provides a medium through which you can carry out research as well as publish your work for an international audience. Students can use word processing, spreadsheet, graphics, photo, audio, and video software to create texts that include words, photographs, drawings, charts and tables, video clips, music and voices. The various elements of a project can be linked together in a nonlinear format by using special Web page design software or by using a coding system called HTML (hypertext markup language). Major software vendors often make shareware packages available on the Internet for you to download and use in developing a project that includes multimedia and hypertext links.

Web projects can be presented just as a traditional paper would, but more often they include a variety of hypertext links. A link on one page may point to a page on the other side of the world, hence the name World Wide Web. In addition, a hierarchy of links can be created that allows readers to move around the project from section to section in a non-linear fashion as they follow their own reading interests and information requirements. You can also include email links for messages from your readers directly back to you, and some software makes the creation of forms very easy. Readers can respond to your survey questions immediately as they read your paper.

With some web development software, forms can easily be created to survey readers and classmates. If you develop this type of project you will need to think carefully about how to structure the material in a fashion very different from the linear nature of a traditional paper. You will also need to remember that while the quantity of information available to you is virtually unlimited and immediate, the quality can vary from totally useless to incredibly important. In the past, sorting out the reliable from the questionable often happened during the lengthy review process that preceded publication of scholarly materials. Now anyone can post anything and you can find your way to it. Careful critical reading and a sense caution are in order.

In addition to the two samples included in this book, there are hundreds of others that you can view by carrying out searches on any number of topics. To get you started, try typing in the following URL (Uniform Resource Locator) or address in your browser: http://www.georgetown.edu/bassr/final.html You'll find a sample of what's available on the Web, and you'll actually be able to follow the links that the students have built into their papers.

Process Writing for "Jammin' in the Apple: NYC Jazz—Bebop to Free"

The process of designing and producing a multimedia project is generally one of collaboration. Often in a professional production, a team is composed of various specialists: graphic designers, researchers, programmers, sound designers, producers, etc. As students, without the benefit of reams of past accolades, our team made quick assessments of each other's skills and divided the tasks accordingly.

We were to create an interactive CD-ROM, Web Sight or Information Kiosk using Macromedia's Director software and we had about six weeks to do it. We started the project with a brainstorming session. Using the time limitations and assignment parameters as a springboard, we started brainstorming for good ideas. I think my idea for an educational CD-ROM about the jazz history of NYC got the nod because it was an idea I had been pushing around since I saw my first educational CD-ROM. I knew that there is a wide breadth of information available both in print and online to aid in our research. And of course, I love jazz. This passion for a topic cannot be understated. When embarking on a project that could very likely have you huddled over a computer monitor with coffee brewing at 2:00 AM, you should make sure you have at least a passing interest in the subject matter.

There has never been a time or place where jazz has undergone as many variations and revolutions as it did in New York City between roughly the years of 1940 and 1965. Schools of musical thought developed and breakthrough players emerged. Influences were passed on, traditions obeyed and broken—all in one place and in one block of time. We felt this provided ample fodder for an interesting project.

Once we decided on our subject, we started to consider our "treatment." How would we treat our subject? Who was our audience? If this were a commercial venture, who would be shelling out cash to buy it? How would we appeal to their interests? We felt that our target audience would be young adults and older people with a passing interest in jazz, or perhaps people who like jazz but don't know what to buy when they walk into a record store. By putting artists in an historical context, providing a brief biography, playing a musical tack and listing a selected discography of their work, the project just might give people a deeper appreciation of jazz and whet their appetites to listen and learn more.

We considered a number of different angles, from purely informative—like an interactive encyclopedia—to a virtual jukebox that would focus mainly on the records of the period. Ultimately we settled on a little of both. We decided to present the material as a virtual trip back in time. Through the means of a photographic slideshow introduction set to appropriate music, we would set the tone for the project and establish the details of time and place. The viewer would see black and white images of New York City's past. Landmarks and street scenes intermixed with occasional performance shots of jazz legends would convey the "feeling" of New York in the middle of this century, putting what would follow into a particular context.

After the slideshow, the viewer is confronted by an alley wall, lit by a single overhead spotlight with four posters advertising a number of performances taking place that evening at actual clubs of the period. This "homepage" essentially represents the thesis of the piece. The four events and artists mentioned as "Coming Soon" on each bill represent the four major schools of jazz in New York between the forties and sixties: Bebop, Hard Bob, Cool and Free Jazz. This page lays out the major structural elements of the project. From here the user can begin to learn and experience the subtleties of each of those schools.

Users, for example, who decide to go to the Open Door club to see the headline act of Charlie Parker, will, after a brief audio-visual interlude through the streets of New York, enter the lobby or a club where they can either enter a door to see a brief video of Parker playing or stay in the lobby and learn about four other prominent Beboppers. Each club has one video performance and four other artists associated with the given school of jazz. Each artist is given his own page with a brief biography describing his place in history, his influences and an explanation of how they fit into a particular school of jazz. As the user reads, a musical selection that exemplifies the musician's style plays in the background. From there, one can go one level deeper to view a photo album or see a selected discography. At all times there is the option to go back a level, go to the lobby or return to the alley.

Once we had this layout conceived, we created a rough storyboard. Each page was sketched on a piece of paper and then laid out in a hierarchical fashion. Then we started to list all of the elements we needed in order to see the project to completion and consider the kinds of resources we could use to do so. We needed vintage images of New York City. We needed images of the artists, as well as digitized recordings of their songs and at least four video clips of live performances. We needed a number of graphical elements such as brick walls, exit signs, lobbies, stages and various buttons for user interaction. And of course we needed a tremendous amount of information about jazz history.

Our greatest resources were ultimately the library and the Internet. My own knowledge of jazz provided a fairly decent springboard, but I found a number of jazz history books to be invaluable. Libraries also have jazz CD collections that can be checked out and digitized using any number of sound editing software titles. The Internet provided many images, including album covers and a few live performance shots. Some kind souls post photographs of musicians from their own collections. Many record labels have impressive websites. These contain lots of information about the artists, discographies, album covers and links to other jazz-related sights. Some search engines like Lycos have the ability to search strictly for pictures and sounds. We created most of the buttons and graphical elements ourselves using Adobe PhotoShop. Video footage was taken from jazz documentaries from the local video store, then digitized and edited in Adobe Premiere.

Once we had done the research, we compiled it along with the various media materials into a functioning CD-ROM educational presentation using Macromedia Director, a fairly elaborate interactive authoring program. This was done largely by my teammate, Travis Luken, whose role as the nuts and bolts technician of the project had clearly defined itself. After a few last minute scramblings for assorted images and a few test runs our project was finally done and ready for viewing by our professor, Robert Hutchinson.

Thad Scott

Nonlinear Project

This project relies heavily on images to create a sense of time and setting as well as to provide audio and visual information about musical artists. There is less text than in a traditional research paper because of the role of sound and image in conveying information. A student could certainly choose to provide fewer visual and auditory components and concentrate more heavily on text. Students working directly with Web page design software would be able to use similar presentation principles—links, text with images, sound—but in a simpler form, at least for now, while the software becomes more user friendly and accessible to a wider range of users.

This project provides information about four schools of jazz and individual information about twenty different musicians. For each school, one musician is featured in a video clip as well as the other information that is consistent among all twenty. The careful hierarchical organization of the pages with logical links among them is an important aspect of coherence within the project. Unlike a print text that is read by everyone in the same order, a text with hyperlinks can be read in many different orders, depending on the choices of the reader.

As the citations indicate, much of the resource material came from Internet sources. Many of the sites did not include much information about who created the material or when it was originally posted or last revised. Thad and Travis have been careful to give credit for the sources on a Works Cited page, which was created after the completion of this project. If they were to begin again, they would need to find a way to develop a button with links to the Works Cited page as well.

Thad and Travis' multimedia research project (a sample of which begins on the next page) includes internal links among the pages. If they were to copy this project into a Web page, they would be able to add additional links to other related sites such as their own home pages and their sources on the Internet. They could send the project or just the address of the site (URL) to their instructor via email, or turn it in on a Zip Disk or CD-ROM disk. They could also make a hard copy of the various screens they had developed, though the sound and video elements would be lost in the paper medium.

Figures 1-3

The reader of this project opens to scenes of New York City. If it is viewed online and if the viewer has a sound card, jazz music will accompany the images. The Admit One ticket in the corner functions as the "button" that "turns" the page. Admit One allows the viewer to skip the introduction completely and move directly to the alley as seen in Image 4.

Fig. 1. Images scanned from Feininger and Lyman.

Fig. 2. Images scanned from Feininger and Lyman; *Jazz Times*.

Figure 4

This image of an alley includes posters of four nightclubs that represent four different schools of music and the musicians associated with each of them. It functions as the entrance point to many different links within the project. By pointing to and clicking on a poster, the reader goes to the "lobby" of that particular club. Here, the viewer sees five photographs, each one providing a link to a biography page or to a video clip of the featured artist. The biography page has a stylized backdrop and a set of links to a discography or a photo album. In each of these areas the user can also hear the music of the artist.

The Exit sign serves as a button to exit the program, and the NYC button takes the viewer back to the alley.

Fig. 3. Images scanned from Feininger and Lyman.

Fig. 4. Images scanned from Berendt *A Photo History*; *Jazz Times*.

Figures 5 and 6

Having clicked on Zoot Sims' picture in Figure 5, the reader moves to the link with the Sims biography page, Figure 6.

The background images for the biography pages were inspired by the artist's record albums and modified by the student writers. The sources for the original images are cited after the abbreviation, <u>Fig.</u> for <u>figure</u>.

Fig. 5. Image of Miles Davis scanned from Abe; Mulligan and Konitz from Avery; Baker from Baker and Pepper.

ZOOT SIMS
There was a fork in the road of the evolution
of the tenor saxophone. At that fork stood
saxophonists Lester Young and Coleman Hawkins.
The two roads of influence continued logically
on into the fifties. The Hawkins road at that
time was dominated by Sonny Rollins, whose
playing still included the big, reedy, almost harsh
tone of his idol. In the other road was a
number of players, including Zoot Sims.
In their playing was the breathy, swinging,
melodic style of Lester Young. Sims' sound
was melodic, soft and laying back on the beat.
Sometimes lumped into the Cool school because
of their relaxed sound, Sims and his ilk were
more about history and most of all, swing.

Fig. 6. Backdrop design based on cover art, Zoot Sims--Quartets.

Figures 7
By clicking the Photo album button on the Zoot Sims biography page, the reader moves to this set of photos of the artist. New choices include the Discography button and the arrow to return to the biography page.

Unity is created by developing language and icons for the buttons that are related to the subject matter of the project and that provide logical links.

Figure 8
Having clicked the Discography button (Fig. 7), the reader moves to this selected discography that highlights major albums of the artist.

From these pages, the lobby button takes the reader back to the lobby of the club, the Photo Album button links to additional pictures and NYC returns the reader to the alley.

Overall Comment

This project provides a model of how technology can enhance the presentation of information through the use of multiple media. It also serves to illustrate that no matter what the medium of presentation, the research process is very similar and the requirements for selecting and focusing a topic, conducting significant and careful research, organizing, developing and documenting sources are consistent with a paper presentation.

The documentation for these images has been added to these sample pages, as has a "Sources Cited" page at the end. While this project was completed and turned in on a CD-ROM disk, it could also be submitted via the web. Naturally a hard copy would omit much of interest—the links as well as the music and video clips would be unavailable to the reader.

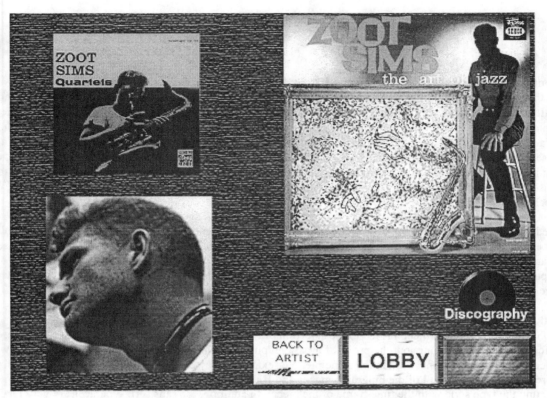

Fig. 7.   Zoot Sims album image on right scanned from *The Art of Jazz*.
          Zoot Sims album image on left scanned from Prestige LP 7026.
          Zoot Sims photo scanned from Ray Avery.

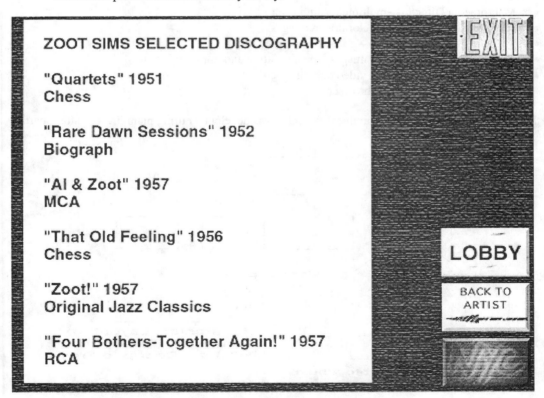

ZOOT SIMS SELECTED DISCOGRAPHY

"Quartets" 1951
Chess

"Rare Dawn Sessions" 1952
Biograph

"Al & Zoot" 1957
MCA

"That Old Feeling" 1956
Chess

"Zoot!" 1957
Original Jazz Classics

"Four Bothers-Together Again!" 1957
RCA

Documentation Format

Because the project was completed as a class project in visual communications to demonstrate the students' ability to use software to develop a multimedia educational presentation, Thad and Travis did not initially incorporate documentation. However, they have since tackled this problem and settled on MLA style documentation with Columbia Online Style (COS) for the electronic resources. COS is a new system for citing electronic sources and can be used with any standard style such as MLA, APA and CBE. The format for the citations resembles that of each standard style. However, you may find it difficult to find all of the information in the online document, in which case, you should come as close as you can to the guidelines. Check with your instructor before using COS for your paper.

They needed to make decisions about how and where to place this documentation in this new medium where the reader doesn't follow a pre–established order as in a traditional paper and where some of the original images served as inspiration for their own "paraphrasing" of them for this project. They have settled on identification of the images on each page with a separate "Sources Cited" page because both print and non-print sources have been included. This page would need to be linked to other places in the document—perhaps with a "Credits" button.

Font and Layout

The graphical nature of this project has led to the selection of a variety of fonts. However, Scott and Travis used the various fonts consistently throughout the project for parallel purposes wherever they occur so that the reader would experience them as an additional organizing principle. For example, they chose New York for the title page for obvious reasons, Geneva for all of the biography pages and Helvetica on the Lobby pages. Their choice was related to connecting the type style with the time frame of the piece. In addition, the sans serif typefaces are very readable over brightly colored graphics.

Software Used:
- Macromedia Director—multimedia authoring
- Macromedia Freehand—vector drawn images
- Macromedia Sound Edit 16—sound sampler, editor
- Adobe PhotoShop—digital imaging, manipulation and import of scans
- Adobe Premier—digitizing video editing video
- Netscape Navigator—web browser

Because the links are non-linear, the hierarchical structure was developed during planning as a storyboard.

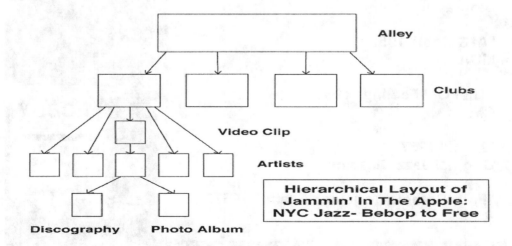

Sources Cited

Abe, Kobo. *Jazz Giants: A Visual Retrospective*. (out of print and publication details unknown)

The Art of Jazz. New York: Seeco Records. (out of print)

Avery, Ray. *The Jazz Photography of Ray Avery II*. http://www.book.uci.edu/Jazz/ and

          http://www.book.uci.edu/Jazz/CDLists/SimsZoot_CDL.html (Nov. 1997).

Baker, Chet, and Art Pepper. *The Route*. Pacific Jazz CDP 7 92931 2.

Berendt, Joachim E. *A Photo History*. New York: Shirmer Books, 1979.

---. *The Jazz Book: From Ragtime to Fusion*. Westport, CT: Lawrence Hill & Co., 1975.

Feininger, Andreas, and Susan E. Lyman. *The Face of New York: The City—How It Was and As It Is*. New York:

          Crown Publishers, 1954.

Goldberg, Joe. *Jazz Masters of the 50s*. New York: The Macmillan Co., 1965.

Jazz Times: America's Jazz Magazine June, 1997: throughout.

Jazz Central Station. Music Boulevard 1998. http://www.jazzcentralstation.com (Nov. 1997).

Lyons, Len. *The 101 Best Jazz Albums: A History of Jazz on Records*. New York: William Morrow Co., 1980.

Marsh, Graham, and Glyn Callingham. *New York Hot . The Album Cover Art*. San Francisco: Chronicle Books,

          1993.

Parent, Bob. *Jazz Photos by Bob Parent*. Bob Parent Archive Project Sept. 1997.

          http://www.allaboutjazz.com/gallery/oct97.htm (Oct. 1997).

Schindelbeck, Frank. "Jazz Links." *The Jazz Pages*. Jazz Institut Darmstadt.

          http://www.jazzpages.com/linkfr_e.htm (Nov. 1997).

Sims, Zoot. *Prestige*. LP 7026. Berkeley: Fantasy, Inc. 1951.

Ulanov, Barry. *A Brief History of Jazz in America*. New York: DeCapo Press, 1972.

WNUR-FM. *People in Jazz*. Northwestern University. http://www.nwu.edu/WNUR/jazz/artists/ (Oct. 1997).

The greatest difficulty I had with the web-project was understanding the fundamental difference between a web-project and a standard paper. I had always thought of writing a paper in linear terms. I can remember being taught in high school that a paper should be thought of in circular terms, but physically speaking, every paper had a beginning, a middle, and an end. I was used to introducing a topic and then building up evidence to arrive at a conclusion.

In working with the web page, however, the concept of using the main idea as the focus of the paper is physically unavoidable. I was forced to ask myself, "How does this idea relate back to the main thesis of the paper?" This is a question that can be brushed aside in standard papers, as one tangent can easily lead to another tangent. In the end, the web-project helped me focus my ideas so I could say what I wanted to say.

Another difficult aspect of the paper was linking my project to the projects of other students. There was an inclination on my part to want to work in a vacuum and link my project to the others when I was finished. However, I found that in working with other students while I was working on my project, connections between the papers were made and ideas came up that I wouldn't have thought of if I hadn't consulted my peers before finishing the project.

Peter J. McMahon

These sample pages from a web project illustrate a number of features that are commonly incorporated in Web Projects. Pete has included internal as well as external textual links, a button bar to connect the pages of his project and graphics. If you read the paper online <http://www.georgetown.edu/users/mchahopj/fppjm1.htm>, you will be able to read the entire project and use these links.

By clicking on any of the underlined text, which appears in blue online, the reader can move to other locations. This allows each reader to move through the paper in a unique order that satisfies personal interests and needs for additional detail on a particular topic.

The Heading

The underlined text in the heading provides links to Pete's homepage, to the class pages of the course professor, and to Georgetown University's home page. Each of these sites would have additional links to related sites, which have links to other sites, and so on.

Paragraph 1

The introductory paragraph provides a link to Professor Randy Bass' "Course Prospectus" and to the syllabus for the course, "American Literary Traditions." Pete uses a quotation from the assignment to set up the focus for the paper. The final lines in the paragraph set up the structure of the project by providing links to other sections that focus on *Racial Masks* and *Cultural Meaning*. These links are further facilitated through the button bar at the end of each section.

Paragraphs 2 and 4

In paragraph 2, Pete provides his response to the assignment as he states his thesis. The underlining in this paragraph and in paragraph 4 lead the reader to another section of the project entitled "Why We Hide." This link is also included in the button bar.

Paragraph 3

At this point Pete begins his analysis by focusing on one of the readings for the course, *Moby Dick*.
The entire text can be found on the Web. Pete has used links as a way of documenting his source. By clicking the words, *Chapter 36*, the reader moves to the particular page of *Moby Dick* where the quotation he has used can be found. Alternatively, he might have used Columbia Online Style guidelines for documenting these sources. Be sure to find out what your professor prefers.

Behind the Masks
by
Peter J. McMahon
American Literary Traditions
Georgetown University
Final Project
Fall 1997

In the Course Prospectus of American Literary Traditions, Professor Randy Bass argues the books in his class "**have some kind of question or problem at the center of them, and that one way to see that problem is as a troubling question about "America" as a place of struggle between ideals and reality, a place where there is a deep and abiding *unanswered promise* that in various forms has political, racial, religious, moral, economic, and cultural meaning.**"

Very often, the "unanswered promise" of America is hidden by the masks people wear. This question is particularly interesting in America, considering the diversity of the American people. The concept of mask can be analyzed on a personal level, but it also provides much insight into the traditions that construct American literature. It is not very often in life that what you see is what you get. In this sense, the American novel is very much like the people it represents. Underneath the surface there is much more going; these goings on encapsulate what it is that makes up the American identity. Novels therefore enable us to search for what is behind the masks people wear and attempt to find meaning in this search.

Herman Melville gets to the heart of this notion in his great American novel, Moby Dick. In Chapter 36, Ahab has the crew of the *Pequod* gathered on the Quarter-Deck. As Ahab explains to them their mission, the reader can get a tremendous sense of Ahab's unquenchable thirst to kill the great white whale. Starbuck questions Ahab's motives, arguing, "**To be enraged with a dumb thing, Captain Ahab, seems blasphemous.**" Ahab responds, "**Hark ye yet again,--the little lower layer. All visible objects, man, are but as pasteboard masks. But in each event --in the living act, the undoubted deed--there, some unknown but still reasoning thing puts forth the mouldings of its features from behind the unreasoning mask. If man will strike, strike through the mask!**"

We find that Ahab's quest is much deeper than simply killing a whale. On the surface, Ahab's mission may seem foolish, but he is driven by something much deeper than simply killing a whale. Everyone else seemed to be missing the point. While the crew may have thought of Moby Dick as just a whale, to Ahab this whale symbolized the quest of a lifetime. Yet no one else seemed to understand the depth at which Ahab was speaking. Despite the apparent madness of his crusade, Ahab was able to see through the pasteboard masks, which most people will never look past and found a higher cause he deemed worth fighting.

Paragraph 6
In this paragraph Pete has used the project of another student in his class as a source. He again documents through building links to the original site. Just as with any other source, Pete provides an analysis of the idea and connects the source to his own paper as he concludes this section.

One of these questions at the center of the human existence is the dichotomy between the person others see us to be and the genuine qualities that truly make us who we are. Everyone puts on a mask at some time or another, in order to hide some thought, feeling, or quality from the world. Masks are very often used as the shrouds which cover up the unique mysteries that define the human experience. In this project, I will look at the various ways in which the structure and form of the novel attempt to get behind these masks and provide the reader with a deeper understanding of the things that make Americans what they are and therefore what America is. We must, as Ahab challenges us, recognize the masks and learn to see past them.

In her project *How the Unspeakable is Revealed in American Novels* Kirsten Catanzano writes, **"American society is obsessed with the idea of "lifting the veil" to reveal the truth. It is thought that if you can expose the truth, then you can fix the problem and salvage the future."** She writes this in the context of the writer's quest to get the 'full story' and in some way **"inch themselves closer to a truer understanding of slavery and the Holocaust."** While I agree with her assessment, there is a more dangerous mask than the kind put on to hide things from *other people*. The most dangerous type of mask is the one that hides things from *ourselves*. This mask therefore prevents us from seeing ourselves as the individuals, the cultural groups, and the nation that we truly are. In this sense, the novels we read in class shine a spotlight on the different masks worn in this country. These novels enable us to stare at the surface and peer into the depths of America.

Why We Hide | The Cultural Mask | The Racial Mask

Behind the Masks

The reader arrives at this section of the project by clicking on "The Cultural Mask" button at the bottom of any section or by clicking on linked related key words within other sections of the text. A different focus on the concept of masks is developed here by analyzing another text from the course.

In this case, Pete begins with a quotation from a printed text of *Ceremony* and the page number is noted in parentheses at the close of the quote. Because everyone in this class has the same edition of the text, the other bibliographic details have been omitted. His use of boldfaced type for the quotations is idiosyncratic to this course.

Paragraph 1
The opening paragraph serves to identify the particular focus of the section as well as to link the discussion of *Moby Dick* with this focus on Leslie Marmon Silko's *Ceremony*.

Paragraph 2
The link to the Austgen article contains a typographical error: <u>while</u> should be <u>white</u>. Pete has noted that the error is in the original by inserting the abbreviation [sic] to let the reader know that the error is in the original. Normally the [sic] would appear immediately after the error, but since this a link, the entire phrase must be rendered as it is in the original.

The Cultural Mask

Behind the Masks
by
Peter J. McMahon
American Literary Traditions

> "They are afraid, Tayo. They feel something happening, they can see something happening around them, and it scares them . . .They think that if their children have the same color of skin, the same color of eyes, that nothing is changing." She laughed softly. "They are fools. They blame us, the ones who look different. That way they don't have to think about what has happened inside themselves" (Silko 100).

One of the great problems America has struggled with is how to unite a culturally diverse country. In this largely immigrant nation, we often discuss the extent to which one can retain a previous country's culture while being able to fit in with the new American identity. Sadly, this question has been largely ignored from the point of view of the Native Americans, who lived on the land long before "America" was created. We find this question of Native American identity encountered in *Ceremony*. The above passage is a stinging indictment of American cultural attitudes towards people who are different--quite an enigma in a land where the 'white' Europeans were the actual newcomers. In *Ceremony*, we find that whites were unable to see their own cultural problems because they could not look past the pasteboard masks of which Ahab speaks. All the while a continuous change was going on behind these masks, and few white people ever saw it.

In an article on the novel entitled, Leslie Marmon Silko's *Ceremony* and the Effects of While Contact on Pueblo Myth and Ritual, [sic] Suzanne M. Austgen addresses what happened when the Laguna Pueblo boys were given the 'American mask' to put on as they served the country in war. She argues, "**Rather than giving the men a new life, World War II destroys them. Rocky is killed fighting the Japanese, Emo becomes an alcoholic, and Tayo returns with a severe case of** <u>**post-traumatic stress disorder that white medicine has been unable to cure**</u>**. In his search for healing, Tayo first turns to drinking with Emo and the other Indian veterans.**"

When Tayo returned from the war, he found ephemeral pleasure in drinking and having people respect him as an American war veteran. In some way he was proud to be able to hide behind the mask of the soldier's uniform. He observed, "**White women never looked at me until I put on that uniform, and then by God I was a U.S. Marine and they came crowding around . . . They never asked me if I was Indian**" (Silko 40). There was something comforting in not being looked down upon or discriminated against because of his Laguna Pueblo heritage. But Tayo found there was no lasting comfort behind the mask of a society that never accepted him--of a society that destroyed him and his people. Tayo could brag about killing the Japanese or his drinking and female exploits, but like the bottom of the beer bottles he stared into, there was nothing but emptiness in the American culture Tayo attempted to hide behind.

Augsten continues, " . . .**becoming part of a pattern of drinking and violence never before witnessed among Indian veterans only makes Tayo sicker. Rather than telling traditional stories about the people's relationship with the earth and the deities, the Indian veterans tell stories about the witchery of the modern world, which has tricked them into believing it is good, just as the Ck' o' yo magician tricked the Pueblos into believing his magic was enough to sustain life.**" Wearing the mask of 'white' culture was draining the life out of Tayo. He eventually finds redemption in what is behind the mask, in the traditions of the Laguna people. He finds there is peace in being himself and seeking his own heritage. This search for himself and his people gives him a satisfaction with which white culture was only tempting him.

Overall Comment

These sample pages from Pete's project demonstrate how links can enhance the development of tangentially related ideas without creating the type of distraction that lengthy footnotes sometimes do. Students can focus on the structural elements of their writing as well as the conceptual links as they decide which elements to join together. Nonlinear papers present the writer and reader with a new type of coherence and transition that emerges from the logic of the connections that are built into the web page organization and from the individual links within the paper.

Documentation Format

With the exception of identifying the source of the graphics in the project, Pete has relied mainly on links to online materials to fulfill the reader's need for references to sources. The two parenthetical notes illustrated here represent an incomplete version of MLA documentation since no "Works Cited" page was developed. More traditional documentation may be required in your courses. Check with your professor.

Font and Layout

The project has been written in 10-point Times New Roman, a very common font that translates well from one computer to another. The use of colored text draws attention to the links that will enable the reader to move easily from one web site to another. The use of Italics, horizontal dividing lines and different font sizes for the title materials emphasizes and sets them off from the text. Scanned images reinforce the content of the project.

In Tayo's communion with the Native American ceremonies and traditions, we find there can be unity amongst the American people because of its diversity. Underneath the surface of American culture is a continually evolving nature that gains its strength from the various proud and lasting traditions of America's many different peoples.

(The Runaway by Tommy Montoya)

Why We Hide | The Cultural Mask | The Racial Mask

Behind the Masks

**Process Writing for "Role Strain and Coping Strategies
On the Family Farm: The Impact of the 1980s Farm Crisis"**

My paper on the American Farm Crisis' effect upon family farmers was a requirement for an occupational sociology course taught by Dr. William Snisek, Alumni Distinguished Professor of Sociology at Virginia Tech. All semester the class read and discussed articles written by other scholars about different occupations. We studied role strain caused by conflicting occupational expectations, coping mechanisms employed by practitioners, similarities and differences between various occupations, and so forth. We were able to generalize the findings of these studies to other occupations and life situations.

At first, I couldn't find much up-to-date information about my topic at all. I scoured the university library, including the electronic databases (FirstSearch, Lexis/Nexis, etc.) and the CD-ROM databases (including Broadcast News), but managed to find only a little information. Finally, I went to the agricultural extension office near my home for help. I was able to get on their on-line computer and access the databases of agricultural colleges all over the country, allowing me to conduct a very thorough review of the most recent research. (The extension agent said that many counties have this kind of resource, but that it is generally under-utilized by the community.)

I originally intended to study the family farm in terms of its desirability compared to other, more industrialized occupational situations. However, as I reviewed the literature, I found the opposite was true. As I indicated in my paper, the interviews I conducted with farm families confirmed my belief that family farming was accompanied by a great deal of role stress and disaffection. Needless to say, I changed the angle of my paper.

In conducting interviews of my own with farmers and their families, I also found that interview technique is very important for accurate results. I'd studied the interview process in detail in my communication research class, and had prepared well for the interviews. However, I soon made a new discovery. In my case, it was essential that I keep the interview sessions strictly one-on-one. Wives and children would give comments and insights they wouldn't ordinarily give when the husband was present and vice-versa.

Tara M. Tuckwiller

Running Head: ROLE STRAIN

Role Strain and Coping Strategies

on the Family Farm:

The Impact of the 1980s Farm Crisis

by

Tara M. Tuckwiller

Virginia Polytechnic Institute

Paragraphs 1-4

Tara introduces her thesis by letting readers know that she had started her research with a hypothesis that the evidence did not support, immediately gaining credibility as an honest researcher and writer. She notes that much of her research was done in the field; such a statement should be included in APA papers whenever primary research is used to support the paper's conclusions. Tara introduces her analysis of role strain, and previews the first major section of the paper by suggesting a "strong" relationship between the Farm Crisis and role strain in farm family members. Because the relationship she is trying to establish is complex, Tara wisely does not claim that the Farm Crisis was the sole cause of increased role strain. Note that Tara has two main threads in her argument: the first is that family members experience three main types of role strain, and the second is that the Farm Crisis partly caused role strain or at least increased its occurrence.

Role Strain and Coping Strategies on the Family Farm:
The Impact of the 1980S Farm Crisis

I first decided to study occupational roles on the family farm[1] because, having lived and worked on a fourth generation farm all of my life (as well as holding several different outside jobs), I have noticed that work roles are perceived and carried out differently in a family farm situation than in most other occupations. I had originally intended to compare family farm work roles with work roles in more industrialized occupations, with the hypothesis that the family farm would produce a more desirable work situation.

I began a review of prior research which had been conducted on farm families, and also conducted some interviews of my own with farm families in the West Virginia-North Carolina area (I interviewed 16 farmers and their families in all). To my surprise, my findings did not support my original hypothesis to any significant extent. However, another pattern began to emerge with regard to the farm family pattern of Role Strain.

For the purposes of this study, I have identified three categories of role strain which appear to be most predominant among farm families. One is Role Conflict, in which the roles one is required to occupy due to different statuses (mother, worker, etc.) do not fit well with each other. Another is Role Frustration, in which there is a poor fit between sociocultural expectations and the opportunity provided by the situation. The last is Role Inadequacy, in which one finds it difficult to perform an expected role because of perceived personal inadequacy.

Through reviewing prior research, as well as studying the history of the family farm, I have concluded that the American Farm Crisis of the early

Headings

Tara divides her paper into several sections with headings to help readers stay focused on her main points, a good idea for papers of more than seven or eight pages. Notice that this heading and the next one, "Role Strain and the Farm Family," are centered, giving readers the visual cue that they are equally important. Subsections are indicated by underlined, flush-left headings. Headings thus act as an outline of the paper.

Paragraphs 5-9

Tara provides the background on the Farm Crisis that readers unfamiliar with the literature will need in order to understand her thesis about the three kinds of role strain experienced by farm families. She uses chronological order to help her readers keep track of an intricate set of historical events leading up to the Farm Crisis, and a cause-effect pattern within each paragraph to build support for her conclusion that the Farm Crisis and role strain are connected. This is a sophisticated treatment that guides the reader carefully through a mass of information.

Paragraphs 6-7

Tara doesn't provide references to her research sources in these paragraphs because this information is common knowledge; any reader could easily verify that her facts are correct.

1980s is strongly related to the recent proliferation of role strain within the farm family. To compensate for their increased financial vulnerability and economic hardships following the Farm Crisis, farm families adopted survival strategies aimed at cutting back expenditures and increasing income. I have found that the emotional tension which is sometimes caused by these very coping strategies, together with the difficulties caused by the financial situation, has revealed and worsened cracks and strains in some aspects of the agrarian ways of life. The purpose of this paper is to demonstrate how certain types of role strain have come to light as a consequence of the Farm Crisis.

The Farm Crisis

The Farm Crisis was a very complex and far-reaching phenomenon to which several books and research projects have been solely devoted. Since understanding the major concepts of the Crisis is essential to the understanding of my discussion about family farms, I will provide a brief overview here.

Due to food shortages in India and the Soviet Union in the early 1970s, American farmers were exporting more food products then ever before. Agriculture's boom years were 1973 and 1974. Many farmers gained confidence as a result of this unprecedented prosperity. They took the opportunity to pay off their earlier debts and took out loans to buy more land, build new and bigger houses for their families, and improve their farm buildings. They bought bigger, more efficient machinery to work the new acres of land. During 1975 and 1976, the food situation in foreign countries began to improve. Farmers received lower prices for their crops, but their situation was still quite good. Expenses were still tremendously high, though,

Paragraphs 8-9

Tara uses the American Psychological Association (APA) in-text citation style to document specific information. In APA style, the author's last name and the publication year of the source are given inside parentheses. When the material is quoted directly from the source, the page number is added to the reference, preceded by p. or pp.

An even more common variation on this standard format is to put the author's name in the sentence, followed by the year of publication in parentheses: *Huntley (1980) describes* .... When the author's name is unknown, a shortened title is substituted, as in the citation to "Hat," which stands for the article "Hat in Hand." Complete publication information for each source is found in the References list at the end of the paper.

particularly for the farmers who were paying off new equipment or new houses. They could continue to make the payments on their loans, but only if crop prices remained high.

But prices plummeted in 1979, when President Carter refused to complete a planned sale of 17 million tons of grain and other food products to the Soviet Union as a way of protesting that country's invasion of Afghanistan. The effects were disastrous for many farmers. For example, the price of wheat fell from $6.00 to $1.80 per bushel. Farmers may have had to spend as much as $3.50 per bushel to raise the wheat (Horwitz, 1980). At the same time expenses continued to rise. In 1979 production costs climbed 7 to 10 percent (Fite, 1981). Farmers were not only paying their operating expenses, but also living expenses for their families, taxes, and the interest and principal on their loans.

What followed was a series of events which (together with the rise and fall of the farming economy, which had already occurred) developed into the Farm Crisis. Increasing need for modern farm technology to match the production standards set by larger corporate farms forced many small farmers to take second and third mortgages on their homes and land, at 17 to 20 percent interest by 1980 (up from 8 percent interest in the 1970s) (Huntley, 1980). Then, due to a drastic $100 billion decline in land values, ("Hat," 1985), loans became harder to obtain since most farmers had traditionally used their land for collateral. As agricultural exports declined, prices continued to fall. Crude oil prices had more than doubled in 1979 ("Rippling Troubles," 1980), creating unusually high fuel expenditures for farmers (the new machinery tended to guzzle diesel fuel). Severe droughts over most of the country lasted from 1980 to 1983, causing many farmers to lose entire crops,

Paragraph 10

Tara explicitly describes the structure of this major section, noting its limitations. Writers often face this same challenge of presenting complicated relationships in a way clear to readers. An alternative solution would have been to divide the material into the three types of role strain and discuss women, children, and men under each type.

Paragraphs 11-13

Tara identifies the main topic of this section: the two types of role strain that farm women experience. In her discussion of the strain resulting from off-farm jobs, she distinguishes between women who were brought up on farms and women who weren't, and then brings the two subgroups back together by noting that 75% of farm women have outside jobs.

Paragraph 12

Throughout the paper, Tara refers to the primary research she conducted. Her judicious use of quotations from her interviews enlivens the paper by showing how individuals describe and attempt to cope with role strain. The quotations also support her main points in an economical way. To ensure confidentiality, Tara does not document the names of the people she interviewed or the dates she talked to them. In cases where sources are not kept confidential, APA recommends to researchers that they offer this information in parenthetical citations in the body of the paper-but not in the References list, where only the sources that other researchers can later retrieve is provided.

Footnotes

Tara uses two footnotes in her paper; the first is on page one. In APA style, footnotes are numbered consecutively throughout the paper (not page by page). Numbers appear in superscript (raised) format. The notes are printed on a separate page at the end of the paper.

season after season. Botched governmental price support programs ended up hurting farmers even more in the long run, especially small farmers.

Role Strain and the Farm Family

I have used subheadings to divide my findings among the different members of the farm family and the types of role strain which affect them most. However, this division is for discussion purposes only. In reality, the strain experienced by the farm owner is intimately connected to the strain experienced by other members of the family, and vice versa. Within each subheading can be found examples of role strain which are so intricately tied to other family members that they could not be separated.

Farm Women

Through my review of others' research and through my own interviews and experience, I have discovered two types of role strain which have increasingly affected farm women since the Farm crisis of the 1980s. One type centers around the woman's off-farm job, and the other centers around the farm crisis' effect upon other family members. These two types of roll strain are intricately interconnected

Some farm wives were raised on family farms themselves, and the traditional farm division of labor has always been their ideal. Working off the farm never crossed their minds until they were forced to look for a way to make ends meet during the Crisis. These women often tried to compensate for this contradiction between their values and economic necessity by practicing role distance. "I'm only working at the feed store (lumberyard, auto parts store) till we can get the farm back on its feet"[2] was an often-heard comment during my interviews. Whether the woman had been working an outside job for six months or six years, she usually explained that it was a "temporary" situation.

Paragraph 14
This paragraph shows the problem Tara had in untangling each of the family members' experiences of role strain.

Other farm wives were not brought up on family farms, or for some other reason don't strongly identify with traditional farm gender roles (in which the woman usually cares for the household but is considered by her husband to be a valuable asset and often, a full partner in the farm business). Many of these women contributed essential financial support by starting full-time outside jobs during the crisis, and have found the experience gratifying. Many continued to work even after the farm had resolved most of its financial difficulties, using the job itself as a coping strategy to help them deal with their lack of identification with the farm and the feelings of worthlessness they associate with the traditional farm wife role.

Regardless of the farm wife's feelings toward her outside job, the reality for 75% of American farm wives is that they must work off the farm for financial reasons (U.S. Department of Agriculture, 1992). This can cause marital strain in some cases, especially if the husband values his traditional role as breadwinner. Husbands who expect to be the sole providers are often uncomfortable when their wives work off the farm because it makes them feel they are "falling down on the job." But many farmers find that they can't really discourage their wives from working outside jobs, because the money the women bring in is usually vitally necessary for the survival of the farm. This contradiction between the sociocultural expectations the farmer feels he must fulfill and the situational constraints which prevent him from doing so results in a sizable amount of role frustration for the farmer, who may then employ different kinds of coping strategies. A man may shore up his perception of the breadwinner role by expressing complete ignorance of his wife's expenditures, thereby implying that her income is used only for insignificant "extras." "I don't know what she does with her money; I really don't!" exclaimed one husband. Or a husband may go the opposite route,

Paragraph 15

Tara indents this long quotation in accordance with APA style, which calls for any quotation longer than 40 words to be set off from the text. Block quotations are indented from the left margin five to seven spaces; the right margin is the same as the text. Note that no quotation marks are used in a block quotation.

Because Tara did not want to reveal the names of her sources, she did not provide parenthetical documentation here. However, all other quotations should be documented. Unlike the citation for a quotation fewer than 40 words in length, the parenthetical citation for a block quotation follows the final period of the last sentence.

Paragraphs 16-17

Tara discusses role conflict, one of the three categories of role strain she has identified. Note that Tara prepares the reader to understand the connections between the quotations and her main point about role conflict by making generalizations. The quotations then offer specific examples of her generalizations. Making explicit statements about how quotations fit into the rest of your paper helps ensure that your readers will draw the same conclusions you did.

Note the bracketed *[original emphasis]* within the quotation at the end of paragraph 16. Tara uses this note to underscore even further the emphasis put on the word "mothering," already underlined. APA doesn't require this kind of a note unless the writer adds emphasis that wasn't in the original, but Tara uses it to good rhetorical effect here. Any time you alter a quotation, you need to show your readers exactly what you changed. Ellipses (three spaced periods) show that you omitted words from within the quotation. Brackets indicate that you added emphasis or added words to make the quotation clear, and the bracketed word [sic] immediately following a word shows that it was misspelled in the original source.

holding his wife accountable for every purchase in order to convince himself and others that he is still in complete control of the family finances. Reports of spouse abuse in farm families have also shown a dramatic increase over the past decade (Bartlett, 1993)—a more destructive type of coping mechanism which frustrated farmers might employ.

Farm women, like other working mothers, may feel that by working outside the home/farm they are neglecting their wife and mother roles. They may feel that they are failing their families by not being there when needed, even though the family's very survival may depend on the mother's paycheck. One mother of two teenagers relates,

> I used to start milking at 4 a.m., do a day's work in town selling
> livestock equipment, then come home and do another milking. I just
> couldn't do justice to both jobs, and I had no energy left to be a
> mother. I took the sales job to provide money for groceries, but I
> wasn't around to guide my children when they needed me, and we have
> lost the communication we had.

As the traditional care giver, the mother frequently is the one who feels a responsibility to hold the family group together. She feels it is her duty to help her family stay close, and may experience role frustration when her situation demands responsibilities which prevent her from fulfilling her personally and socioculturally expected role of primary care giver.

Women who were raised on traditional family farms or in other traditional-style households may feel an obligation or desire to fulfill the roles which their mothers performed and which they, as young girls, were socialized to perform, Often, outside work gets in the way of this goal. One

Paragraph 18
Tara summarizes this section briefly by noting the many responsibilities that farm women have, implying in the last sentence that they experience many more than the two types of role conflict identified specifically.

Paragraph 19
Tara uses an anecdote about a single family to introduce the section on role strain experienced by children. Anecdotes are often effective in getting readers to feel more emotionally involved in the subject.

woman remembered wistfully, "my current hectic lifestyle really leaves me little time for the cooking and <u>mothering</u> (original emphasis] I remember from my own childhood."

Farm women who work off the farm must also contend with the "second shift" (Hochschild, 1989)--the hours of housework and childcare that await them when they arrive home after a full day's work. A farm wife comes home not only to her responsibilities as a wife and mother, but to her duties as a farm worker. To her, home really was another workplace, just as important to the family's financial wellbeing as her outside job. Farm women are usually responsible for many areas of the farm, including care of livestock (especially dairy cows, chickens, and pigs), bookkeeping and keeping track of complicated farm finances, as well as the majority of household chores and helping husbands and children with fieldwork. The sheer diversity of roles a farm wife is expected to perform inevitably leads to a complex web of role conflicts, if not total work overload.

<u>Farm Children</u>

Children can be especially vulnerable to strain caused by their role on the family farm, particularly if they live or attend school in a community where farmers are a minority. In one family, the children pleaded to go without lunch rather then stand in the lunch line and endure the humiliation at the hands of peers and even school faculty. Their parents, unable to provide each child with a dollar for lunch every day, had secured free lunch tickets for the children through a school program. As they passed through the line, the children were required to present the tickets, which

Paragraphs 19-21

Tara takes up the consequences of poverty for farm children. Note her use of "may" in the phrases "may seek to marry early" and "may be one reason." Such careful qualification of relationships she suspects but can't prove add to her credibility for readers.

Paragraph 21

In examining a paper for revision, look closely at very short paragraphs such as Paragraph 21. Their brevity may indicate that you need to add more examples, statistics, or other support for the topic sentence. For example, Tara might have noted that 4 of the 6 teenagers she talked to mentioned their lack of money as a reason for not dating, or offered whatever other support she has for the general statements she makes here. (Other times, integrating a very short paragraph into another, closely related one may help your ideas flow more smoothly.)

Paragraphs 22-24

The first sentence of Paragraph 22 functions as a topic sentence for this whole block of paragraphs.

were bright orange to allow easy identification by the lunch money collector (and unfortunately, by sarcastic peers as well). One teenager who never had the money to purchase snacks at the snack bar reported being taunted by his peers: "You can grow food but you can't buy it."

Children tend to employ some fairly self-destructive coping strategies when faced with conflict. Farm children who are bitter about family poverty (or increasing domestic violence, which will be discussed later) may seek to marry early, and perhaps less carefully, in an effort to escape the farm situation. This practice can result in unhappy and short-lived marriages, and may be one reason for the increasing divorce rate among farm families (Barlett, 1993). Hasty marriages can also result in strained finances, which often means that farm children will have no opportunity to obtain the increasingly desirable college degree, Children are often worried about the whispered discussions their parents have about finances when they think children can't hear, or have anxiety due to the verbal, physical, or emotional abuse they may receive when parents take out their frustrations on the children. In these cases grades usually suffer, and more and more farm children are turning to drugs and alcohol as coping strategies (Barlett, 1993).

When teenage boys begin to want to date, they rarely have cash to spend on dinner, movies, or gas for the car. Even farm teens with part-time jobs usually end up contributing most of their earnings to the upkeep of the farm, with the promise that "this will all be yours someday."

However, farm parents' ability to pass down an intact and financially solvent farm to their children is becoming less and less certain. Children were brought up (especially prior to 1979) believing that they would have a secure and stable future on the farm. They planned to raise their own

families on the family farm, becoming full owners when it was time for their parents to retire (or die). This is the future for which children planned, through the 4-H and Future Farmers of America activities in which they participated, the classes they took in high school, sometimes even the degree they pursued in college. The possibility that this future may not be available to them can result in feelings of hopelessness among young aspiring farmers. One young man, who faces the imminent demise of his short-lived attempt at farming, summed up the feeling of many: "Farming's all I know," he mumbled, staring at the ground. "What am I going to do now?"

More then ever before, an older farmer's sponsorship (usually Dad's) is essential for young men who want to break into the occupation. Even if the newcomer is not actually taking over his father's land, he'll still need plenty of help getting started. The young farmer will need to borrow equipment--a new tractor costs at least $50,000, and it's become quite difficult for new farmers to secure bank loans. If a young farmer wants to have any possibility at all of being granted a loan, he'll need an established farmer's endorsement with the local banker. Ditto for credit at feed or seed stores. However, such sponsorship may not be widely available for several reasons. Established farmers today do not automatically have good credit rating with local banks or stores, as a result of the economic hardships they endured during and after the Farm Crisis. For the same reason, many farmers were forced to sell their own equipment and have been unable to purchase newer, more technologically advanced equipment which newer farmers (who tend to prefer raising specialty crops, such as organic foods) may find necessary to their operation. Due to this lack of available sponsorship, many young farmers end up quitting after a few years or never enter the occupation at all.

What happens when there is more than one heir interested in taking over the family farm operation? Today's small farms are often hard-pressed to provide a living for one family, much less two. But because foreign investors and corporate farming operations have been buying large quantities of American farmland since the 1970s, there is now a shortage of land available for a young farmer who cannot claim the family farm as his own (Gorman, 1987). Even with the aforementioned sponsorship, this lack of available farmland reduces the chance that a young farmer will be able to fulfill his expected role, which leads to role frustration. Obviously, the question of who will take up the reins of the family farm can cause an enormous amount of conflict within the family as well.

Farm children who are eligible for scholarships and financial aid are more likely to pursue a college degree than they were before the Crisis (Gorman, 1987). They cite a desire to get an edge in the knowledge of farming technology and the fact that a degree is often beneficial when it comes to the nearly inevitable off-farm job search as reasons they decided to attend college. But sometimes farm children discover, through the process of getting a college education that their true interests lie elsewhere and that they really don't want to take over the family farm after all. This often results in conflict with parents, who expect the child to enter the farming occupation. Sometimes the child will ignore his own wishes and take over the family farm, resulting in a lifetime of perceived role inadequacy. Sometimes the child will ignore his parents' wishes and enter some other occupation, resulting in a lifetime of family conflict. More often, a child will enter another occupation and will try to manage the family farm on the side, which inevitably results in never-ending role conflicts.

Family Farm Owners

Farmers themselves experience their share of role strain due to the occupation they have chosen. One source of strain for the farmer is related to the prestige his occupation is accorded by society at large. Different prestige is assigned to certain jobs and working conditions, but when workplaces are out of the public view (as is the case with the family farm), prestige is difficult to assess. Claims to status and rank are thus made increasingly through lifestyle, and since most family farm owners can't afford the normal rate of consumerism, they are accorded low prestige by members of the non-farm community. "Farmers are treated as though they live in a shack, have one old pair of overalls and a broken-down pickup truck," complains one reasonably successful, middle-aged farmer.

Although most farmers have been able to maintain their family's standard of living at the pre-Crisis level, few have been able to raise their standard of living much over the past two decades. This was a major source of feelings of role inadequacy for the farmers I interviewed. Many have taken outside jobs in an attempt to stay afloat financially, and there is always farm work to be done in the early morning and evenings. Some have been forced to lay off their hired help, and most must attempt to meet today's productivity standards without the aid of expensive equipment. This creates a great deal of extra work for the farmer himself, and makes it increasingly difficult for him to take an afternoon off to be with a child or to go to a school or church function. This dilemma contradicts the "agrarian work values" (freedom from supervision, flexibility of work pace, etc.) which attracted many farmers to the occupation in the first place.

As mentioned earlier, many farmers have been forced to take jobs off the farm as a result of the financial difficulties caused by the Farm Crisis. This can cause role strain for the farmer, even if he is lucky enough to get an agriculturally-related job (such as selling farm implements or teaching vocational agriculture). No matter what the outside job is, it will almost certainly involve complex relations with coworkers, supervisors, and subordinates, who, importantly, <u>are not family</u>. (Even a job at the local slaughterhouse or lumber mill requires a more complex set of work relations than the farmer is accustomed to.) These conditions can result in feelings of "pressure," "stress," and "hassle" for farmers who are used to independent, solitary work. These men tend to employ the same role distancing strategies as their wives, who often find themselves in similar situations.

Despite the grueling work pace and outside work efforts of farmers, a family farm goes under every six minutes in this country (Comstock, 1987). Although many social factors are conspiring against small farmers, these men tend to feel personally responsible when their land is swallowed up. "When you lose a farm that's been in the family for generation after generation, you feel like a failure," admitted the young farmer mentioned earlier who has been unable to beat the odds. This feeling of worthlessness is often compounded by the attitudes of family members. In some cases, older parents blame their farming children for losing the family farm, believing that they must be lazy or inefficient. Farmer's wives may also blame them for the loss of the farm. "We'd probably still own the land I grew up on if I hadn't married a dreamer," one woman remarked bitterly, after being forced to sell a large portion of her parents' farm when her husband's plan for raising bell peppers didn't work out.

Paragraphs 30-33

Earlier, Tara described some of the strategies women and children use to cope with role strain. In these paragraphs, she discusses some of the (dysfunctional) coping strategies farm owners use when they lose their farms. Some readers might argue that this last discussion, especially, goes beyond Tara's thesis as set up in her introduction. Others, however, will find these paragraphs an especially chilling conclusion to the whole role strain section, and an effective transition to the next section. This block of paragraphs might be shortened so that the material on failed farmers' coping strategies would become less prominent in relation to the main topic, role strain.

Many farmers are willing to sacrifice almost anything, as long as they retain the land that is their heritage. "We're getting by with the aid of food stamps, heating assistance, and any other program that we're eligible for. It hurts our pride, and I guess it injures our dignity, but we're willing to suffer these indignities in order survive with our land intact," one farm wife affirms. Every decision these farmers make is made with the best interests of the farm in mind, because losing the land would simply be too much to bear.

When the unthinkable happens, when farmers are informed that their land will be auctioned by the bank, they tend to employ different kinds of coping strategies. A few farmers withdraw from social interaction. Now that they have no livelihood and no credit with the bank, they avoid going into town to escape seeing friends they can't pay. This may be one reason why rural membership in groups such as the Jaycees, Masons, Extension clubs, and churches has been dropping in recent years (Gorman, 1987). There is a sense of betrayal of trust and loss of friendship, especially when a banker whom a farmer has known and dealt with for decades is forced to foreclose.

Sometimes farmers employ more destructive coping strategies. Day-to-day stress and the sleepless nights, which often follow, can contribute to a high level of frustration among farmers, who are usually characterized by their wives as keeping their problems bottled up inside. More and more farmers are turning to alcohol in an attempt to shut out their problems (Barlett, 1993). As mentioned before, domestic violence in farm families is on the rise--more farmers are battering their wives, children, and elderly parents (Barlett, 1993), and some take out their frustrations on their animals. One veterinarian says that she treats, on a regular basis, family farm dogs that have had their ribs kicked in. In one case, a farmer reacted to a bank loan

refusal by letting twenty-four of his horses simply starve to death.

Farmers can, indeed, be driven to destruction when they are notified that their land is being taken from them. This feeling of powerlessness led one man to turn a loaded shotgun on his neighbors' homes, causing extensive property damage (but, fortunately, no injuries). In another instance, a distraught farmer shot and killed several people before killing himself. His financial troubles were about to claim his farm and everything he owned.

Other failed farmers have also chosen to turn their anger on themselves. According to one University of Missouri sociologist, the suicide rate among farmers is 30 to 40 percent above the national non-farm rate--and rising (Barlett, 1993). Some analysts speculate that there are probably more suicides than is commonly thought, since many are staged to look like accidents so that the farmer's family will be able to collect life insurance benefits. One family farm owner, who had recently been informed of the bank's foreclosure on his farm, announced as his wife was getting his two daughters ready for school one morning that he was going out to shoot groundhogs (a common early-morning pest control practice among farmers) and not to bother holding breakfast for him. Later that day, his body was found beside a fence; he had been killed by a self-inflicted gunshot wound to the stomach. It was determined that it <u>could</u> have happened while the farmer was loading the gun, but many members of the community suspected suicide. However, nobody wanted to stigmatize the family or prompt an investigation which would cost the surviving wife and children precious insurance money. This story is all too common in farming communities, but nobody mentions the word <u>suicide</u> for the reasons listed above. Consequently the phenomenon is underreported and many outsiders don't realize that a problem exists.

Paragraphs 35-38
Tara offers a counterpoint by bringing up the personal motivations her interviewees have for continuing to farm in the face of the many barriers she has just related. She reminds readers that even though role strain is widespread, the negative consequences of farming are only one aspect of a profession many still regard as empowering to the person and important to the community.

So Why Farm?

When one looks at all of the disaffections associated with owning and operating a family farm, it is not difficult to see why farm families find it necessary to adopt various strategies in order to cope. Some farmers, especially new ones, are forced to just give up altogether. But other farmers have managed to stay. Why do these farmers choose to "tough it out?" And what is it about owning a family farm that keeps attracting young people to the occupation?

Popular culture to some extent romanticizes the family farm and minimizes the financial and emotional constraints of running a family enterprise (Fink, 1992). Reverence for the farming life runs deep in our society, and it seems to reflect an appreciation for dimensions of satisfaction (Mooney, 1988) that have been stripped from those who live "up there on the concrete." Some of the positive aspects of owning and operating a family farm reported by interviewees include:

* Personal empowerment and pride in meaningful work, work that clearly serves a wider societal need

* Linkage of work and family, of long-term ties not only to kin but to a like-minded community

* The combination of work and family with place and a sense of attachment to land and region

* The sense that work and play, effort and leisure, flow into each other and grow out of each other

* A sense of daily connectedness to nature and to deeper spiritual realities embodied in the work process

I also found that, in many cases, part of the attraction of farming is the uncertainty of the reward: "I enjoy the challenge of the gamble," one man admitted. Another farmer agreed, "The farm is a dream, and either it comes true or it doesn't. When it comes true, you want it over and over." The

Paragraphs 39-40

Tara concludes her paper by briefly reviewing her findings and then putting her work into the larger context of role strain as it might be experienced in other occupations affected by major economic changes. Often, academic research raises interesting questions others might wish to explore.

Overall Comment

Tara's paper is original in concept and sophisticated in approach, as befits a paper written for a senior class. She clearly and convincingly supports her thesis that farm families are experiencing different kinds of role strain. At the same time, she demonstrates probable causal connections between the Farm Crisis and role strain in the farm family, and explores the coping mechanisms women, children, and men use in response to role strain. These secondary purposes link the sections of the paper into a smooth, coherent presentation.

The fact that Tara conducted extensive primary research without neglecting existing research is also very impressive in an undergraduate paper. Tara used her interviewees' statements as well as information derived from other sources to back up her own intelligent analysis, not to substitute for it. In fact, Tara's instructor called this paper "outstanding, highly publishable."

farmer enjoys matching human wit, skill, and experience against nature, "the experts," and the multinational corporations, sometimes with a good annual return. Some men and women say they dislike the gambling part of farming, but even they volunteer, "it _is_ a good feeling when it turns out good." Many farmers also report a deep sense of unavoidable attachment to farming. They feel that they _must_ work the land, not only because it is their job, but for their own emotional well-being. Most responses tended to be variations on the same theme, summed up nicely by one middle-aged cattle farmer: "Farming is my greatest love--it's the best way of life."

Conclusion

I have attempted to illustrate, through specific examples, how the Farm Crisis of the 1980s has affected farmers and their families. The Crisis caused severe financial difficulties, especially for small farmers. This in turn has revealed and worsened, and in some cased actually caused, several kinds of role stress for members of the farm family. The family has consequently adopted various types of coping strategies in order to deal with the increased stress. Some strategies, such as taking jobs off the farm, have relieved some of the financial stress that resulted from the Farm Crisis but have created new stresses for the farm family in the process. Other strategies, including drug and alcohol abuse, domestic violence, animal abuse, and suicide have actually worked to destroy the farm family and its traditional values.

The dilemma of the farm family can be applied to other occupations as well. Parallels can be drawn between the situation of the small farmer and that of others whose jobs are being affected by shifts in the economy. For example, I believe that it would be interesting to see what effect the shift toward a service economy in America has had on industrial workers (such as

steelworkers or mine workers, whose jobs are very precarious) and their families. Also, with more and more industries setting up operations abroad, some workers (such as garment workers) and their families may be experiencing various kinds of role strain as their jobs are being handed over to cheap foreign labor. And the downsizing of major American corporations such as IBM may have similar effects, both for displaced workers and for workers who have managed to stay with the company. All of these occupations have been affected by economic changes and, like the farm family, the families of these workers may be feeling the effects for a long time to come.

Footnotes

[1]A family farm is an agricultural operation owned and worked primarily by the family, with gross annual sales of less than $40,000 and which hires no more than one permanent non-family worker (Tweeten, 1984). Family farms constitute about 75% of the 2.2 million total U.S. farms (U.S. Department of Agriculture, 1992).

[2]All quoted material comes from the interviews I conducted for this study unless otherwise noted.

Documentation Format

Tara uses the American Psychological Association (APA) documentation system. The sources referred to within the paper are included on a "References" page (except for interviews or other unrecoverable research).

Use the following general rules as a guide in formatting this page:

- Center the heading "References" at the top of a new page.
- Double-space all lines, and indent the second and subsequent lines of each entry five to seven spaces.
- Alphabetize by the main author's last name.
- Sequence the information as follows:
  Book: author, date of publication, title, place of publication, publisher
  Periodical: author, date of publication, article title, periodical title, pages

Font and Layout

Tara produced this paper on a typewriter in a Courier font, setting her margins at one inch and justifying the left hand side of the text. Underlining is used in place of Italics. The document is double-spaced, with major headings in the text centered and minor headings underlined. Raised-numeral endnote references are the same size as the type.

References

Barlett, P. (1993). <u>American dreams, rural realities: Family farms in crisis.</u>

    Chapel Hill, NC: University of North Carolina Press.

Comstock, G. (Ed.). (1987). <u>Is there a moral obligation to save the family</u>

    <u>farm?</u> Ames, IA: Iowa State University Press.

Fink, D. (1992). <u>Agrarian women: Wives and mothers in rural Nebraska,</u>

    <u>1880-1940.</u> Chapel Hill, NC: University of North Carolina Press.

Fite, G. (1981). <u>American farmers: The new minority.</u> Bloomington, IN:

    Indiana University Press.

Irman, C. (1987). <u>America's farm crisis.</u> New York: Franklin Watts.

Hat in hand. (1985, November 11). <u>Time,</u> 71.

Hochschild, A. (1989). <u>The second shift: Working parents and the</u>

    <u>Revolution.</u> New York: Viking.

Horwitz, E. L. (1980). <u>On the land.</u> New York: Athenaeum.

Huntley, S. (1980, May 19). Why farmers are singing the blues. <u>U.S. News and</u>

    <u>World Report,</u> 56.

Mooney, P. (1988). <u>My own boss?: Class, rationality, and the family farm.</u>

    Boulder, CO: Westview.

Rippling troubles from the farm belt. (1980, July 14). <u>Business Week,</u> 94.

Tweeten, L. (1904). <u>Causes and consequences of structural change</u>

    <u>in the farming industry.</u> Washington, DC: National Planning

    Association.

U.S. Department of Agriculture. (1992). <u>The 1992 Yearbook of Agriculture.</u>

    Washington, DC: U.S. Government Printing Office.

Process Writing for "Microsoft Corporation"

Over the year before I wrote this paper, I had developed an interest in Microsoft concerning their trade practices relating to the FTC's investigation, especially the legal aspects. Initially, I wanted to write the paper from a legal perspective. But for the purposes of my marketing class, I was to focus on the issues involved from a marketing perspective, specifically on product development to meet marketing trends.

Since the paper involved a very current situation, I needed information as recent as possible, so I decided to research periodicals and newspaper articles for the information I needed. This increased research and organizational time since so many articles were available. This also presented a change from my previous papers. Rather than researching a limited number of long texts, condensing an abundance of information, I found myself researching a large quantity of short articles, expanding on a limited amount of information. Keeping track of all the articles became much more of a task than I was accustomed to.

In writing the paper, once I determined the format, there were no real hang-ups. I did have a little trouble sticking to the marketing focus because I was so interested in the legal aspects of the topic. On page two it just seemed natural to discuss the criticisms of Microsoft because, in describing its marketing tactics, I had to bring in the idea that they were controversial. But I brought my paper back to marketing on page three by showing how the same companies that criticize Microsoft also indirectly benefit from those same tactics.

I had no problems with the "writer's block" that I had had in the past. Because I was writing about a subject I had an interest in, the research and writing were much easier than usual.

Mike Sill

148

Running Head: MICROSOFT

Microsoft Corporation

Mike Sill

Marketing 3104

Professor Rieley

October 13, 1993

Paragraphs 1-3

These three paragraphs constitute a long introduction, providing background information about Microsoft. Although he knows that much of this information is known by his readers, for the purposes of the assignment, Mike includes it to establish the context for the rest of the paper.

Mike is using the American Psychological Association (APA) documentation system. Like MLA, APA uses in-text references but includes the year of publication and the author's name. Include the page number only if you directly quote the source. As illustrated in paragraph 2, the order of the information in a citation is as follows: author's last name, year of publication, page number (when necessary). Use commas to separate the information, and include "p." in front of the page number. Unlike MLA, running heads should be an abbreviated (one or two word) version of the title, rather than the writer's last name.

Microsoft Corporation

In the world of personal computers, the Microsoft name is well known. The Microsoft Corporation is an industry leader in computer software development. Through aggressive and effective strategic management, Microsoft has become the world's largest and most successful software manufacturer. Its MS-DOS operating system and Windows applications software have become industry standards. With a focus on the future, continually developing innovative products and expanding into new technologies, Microsoft will remain a leader in the computer industry.

Microsoft is not only the largest computer software company in the world, but also the most powerful. Its technological smarts, widely praised management, and aggressive competitive nature have made it a juggernaut influencing almost every aspect of personal computing(Saguaro, 1993). One of the reasons for Microsoft's success has been its MS-DOS operating system. Through a joint venture with IBM, Microsoft was able to establish MS-DOS as the industry standard for IBM compatible applications. Most personal computers are equipped with MS-DOS when sold. It has become the world's most popular operating software, with no close second. It is used on more than 80% of all personal computers (Suqawara, 1993). In addition, Microsoft Windows has had a great influence on the compatibility and accessibility of personal computers.

The computer software industry is extremely competitive. It is a "sink or swim" industry in which Microsoft dominates the competition due to various strengths. In fact, during a recession in which many companies are incurring record lows, Microsoft recorded its first billion-dollar quarter this year, with earnings up 26% and profits up 35%. Also increased were amounts spent on

Paragraph 4

In this transitional paragraph, linking the introduction to the next part of the paper, Mike emphasizes Microsoft's main marketing objective.

Notice that the source cited at the end of the paragraph has a "b" after the year. This indicates that the source Mike has cited here is the second of two sources written by the same author in the same year. The letter is also included with the source on the "References" page.

Paragraph 5

The source that Mike paraphrases does not have an author, so he uses an abbreviated title instead of author's name.

Paragraphs 6-7

As Mike states in his process writing, his personal interest is in the legal aspects of the topic, and here he shifts his discussion a bit to include that interest. However, this section does not seem arbitrarily thrown in to the paper because Mike makes sure to set up the section with a transitional sentence at the end of paragraph 5 mentioning that Microsoft's tactics are "controversial" and "criticized."

research and development, a 20% increase over the previous quarter. Microsoft traditionally spends well above the industry average on research and development (Andrews, 1993a). It makes investments in just about every new technology that appears (Sugawara, 1993).

Though Microsoft emphasizes product development, perhaps an equally crucial ingredient in its success lies in its management strategies and objectives. Rather than complete concern for profitability, founder and chairman Bill Gates emphasizes continually increasing Microsoft's market share within the industry, while maintaining a relentless long-term focus (Andrews, 1993b).

One of its strengths has always been the ability to attract large business. In August of this year, Microsoft signed more than 200 organizations to large--scale volume purchasing and maintenance agreements for Microsoft products ("Microsoft Says," 1993). Microsoft has been able to attract this many customers by utilizing a range of innovative, though controversial, marketing tactics. While its promotional tactics have been widely successful, its pricing strategies and trade practices have been criticized.

Since June of 1990, Microsoft has been under investigation three times by the Federal Trade Commission, and is now under investigation by the Justice Department for anti-trust law violations. It is accused by its competitors of using the market power of MS-DOS to compete unfairly in the software market, and allegedly of building features into its software that made competitors' products incompatible with Microsoft software. Microsoft has also offered large discounts to computer manufacturers if they agreed to pay royalties to Microsoft on every computer shipped rather than sold (Lewyn, 1993). Other allegations include predatory pricing: undercutting the competition by selling products at a loss.

Paragraph 7
Mike uses this paragraph to bridge the discussion of Microsoft's legal troubles with his discussion of Microsoft's development of new products. Transitional phrases at the beginning ("Despite . . .") and at the end Microsoft's own marketing techniques") link the preceding and the following paragraphs.

Paragraph 8
Mike begins the part of his paper that directly addresses the assignment, to discuss the product development of a company in a marketing context.

Paragraphs 8-9
Mike lists and describes the products recently out on the market and those planned for the near future.

Despite allegations of illegal trade practices, not all of Microsoft's competitors hold a grudge. The industry has benefited a great deal from Microsoft. By Microsoft's count, more than 500 companies have emerged just to create software for Windows, resulting in more than 17,000 jobs. In total, more than 16,000 software companies nationwide are involved in developing software for Windows (Sugawara, 1993). Most of these companies are dependent on Microsoft and so are careful to maintain good working relations with the company. The success of many smaller software companies can be traced to their ability to learn from and deploy Microsoft's own marketing techniques (Andrews, 1993b).

Microsoft's domination of the software industry can be largely attributed to its products available for application software and to its ability to secure market shares for these products. Not only is MS-DOS used on over 80% of all computers, a new improved version, MS-DOS 6.0 is now available (Sugawara, 1993). Improvements in the MS-DOS 6.0 utilities include Microsoft MemMaker for memory management, and Microsoft Double-Space for data storage compression, which actively doubles a computer's storage capacity (Ayre, 1993). In addition, Microsoft has developed a new Windows package, Windows 4.0, Windows NT Standard Edition, and Windows for Workgroups (Lindquist, 1993). However, not all of Microsoft's application software has done well. Specialized packages such as Microsoft Money, financial software designed to compete with Quicken, received favorable reviews, but did poorly in the marketplace (Andrews, 1993b).

Another focus of Microsoft is growth and development of new technologies. One of the latest developments in the computer industry is CD-ROM and multimedia computer capabilities. Microsoft has introduced Cinemania, a CD-ROM database for film. Though Cinemania does not offer full animation, it does include authentic movie sound clips (Trivette, 1993).

Paragraph 10

Now Mike begins to explain why some of these products are risky ventures but will most likely succeed because of Microsoft's strategy of innovation and long-range planning. This paragraph picks up on the ideas in paragraph 4 and expands on them.

Paragraph 11

Mike continues to list and describe Microsoft's products, but now focuses on the even more innovative products planned for future. Since these products may be unfamiliar to many readers, even marketing students, Mike could add brief, one-line descriptions of these products.

Microsoft will also soon release its own Open Base Connectivity (ODBC) drivers. ODBC drivers allow access to popular network database servers such as Oracle, dBase, SQL Server and Paradox (Mace, 1993). Soon, Mac users will be able to run IBM PC-compatible software, and vice versa. Microsoft, along with Insignia Solutions, is developing software that will allow Windows to be run directly on a Mac CPU (Rizzo, 1993). For office integration, Microsoft's planned Atworks could provide companies with the convenience of integration through means of a new generation of management applications, uniting data and telephone management, and networking fax machines, copiers, and telephones.

Though most businesses are not equipped for such technologies, this exemplifies Microsoft's commitment to remain ahead of the competition (Derfler, 1993). And while some companies have criticized and questioned Microsoft for designing such products, it is this attitude and belief in innovation and the future that has made Microsoft the industry leader. It has recently been expanding its research efforts in interactive television, movies on demand, integration of office equipment and development of new home devices (Andrews, 1993a). While some of these products may seem useless and unnecessary, this is often the case when technologically advanced products are first introduced. Products such as microwaves and VCR's received similar criticism during the developmental and introductory phases of their product life cycles, just as digital audio tape is currently.

As for the future of Microsoft, it is working together with communications equipment manufacturers to develop Microsoft's Digital office Project, and is examining how people create and move documents and how to improve the process. Bill Gates expects the fastest areas of growth within the computer industry to be pen computing, CD-ROM, corded telephone use, and flat screen technology. Frontiers Microsoft will work on ways to combine computing and communications and on artificial intelligence (Kirkpatrick,

Paragraph 12
The paper ends with a brief closing statement which summarizes the paper, emphasizing Mike's conclusion that Microsoft will continue to do well.

Overall Comment
Mike's paper is soundly documented to show how Microsoft's product development relates to its long-range marketing strategies. The limitations of the topic most likely created some problems for Mike because, though the paper adequately addresses the assignment, it basically passes along information gathered from the sources. Mike's fluent writing style shows that he is a logical thinker and, despite the "writer's blocks" he says he sometimes has, is generally comfortable writing. He probably would have been able to write a livelier paper if he had been allowed to choose the approach to the topic he was most interested in.

1993). Two key trends in shaping Microsoft's environment over the next decade will be dramatic increases in micro-processing power, and a gigabit-per-second fiberoptic network linking every business and home. Windows will be adapted for systematic multi-processing and 64-bit computing (Davis, 1992).

With its focus on the future and continual commitment to research and development of new products and technologies, Microsoft will continue to grow and succeed. Effective strategic management has played a key role in its success, with strong commitment to long-term planning, promotion, and competitiveness. Through product innovation and aggressive marketing, it will continue to dominate the computer software industry.

Documentation Format

Mike uses the American Psychological Association (APA) documentation system. The sources used in the development of the paper are included on a "References" page (except for interviews or other unrecoverable research). Use the following general rules as a guide in formatting this page:

- Center the heading "References" at the top of a new page.
- Double-space all lines, and indent the second and subsequent lines of each entry five to seven spaces.
- Alphabetize by the main author's last name.

Notice that the years for the two Andrews citations are followed by a lower case a and b respectively. This shows the reader that the citations come from different issues during the same year of the same periodical.

Font and Layout

This manuscript was produced on a typewriter, with double spacing and one-inch margins justified on the left-hand side.

References

Andrews, P. (1993a, July 29). Microsoft tops $1 billion. The Seattle
Times, p. C25.

Andrews, P. (1993b, August 26). Quick study on Microsoft marketing aids
success. The Seattle Times, p. C21.

Ayre, R. (1993, September 14). Microsoft MemMaker. PC Magazine, 130-31.

Davis, D. (1993, September 15). Future quest: Microsoft Corporation.
Datamation, 42.

Derfler, F. and Greenfield, D. (1993, September 14). Atworks: The future
of integrated technology? PC Magazine, NE75.

Kirkpatrick, D.(1993, June 28). How Bill Gates sees the future.
Fortune, 10.

Lewyn, M. and Rubello, K. (1993, May 3). The Microsoft probe looks
like a bust for trustbusters. Business Week, 32.

Lindquist, C. (1993, July 26). Microsoft, get it together. Computerworld,
37-8.

Mace, S. & Barney, D. (1993, July 5). First pack of ODBC drivers finally
shipping. InfoWorld, 1-2.

Microsoft says more than 200 firms sign large purchase pacts. (1993,
August 10). Dow Jones News Service, Story 122 (on-line).

Rizzo, J. (1993, October). The multi-use Mac. MacUser, 133-35.

Sugawara, S. (1993, August 29). Microsoft: Hot rod or road hog? The
Washington Post, Financial, p. Bl.

Trivette, D. (1993, January 12). Microsoft's Cinemania on CD-ROM. PC
Magazine, 485.

Process Writing for "Contributions of Women during the Roman Era"

Writing this research paper was both challenging and rewarding. Most of the challenges and all of its success were directly related to the co-authoring of this piece. The challenge of bringing together unique perspectives, fending off time constraints, and sharpening the focus of the paper through careful elimination of non-essential diction brought great satisfaction to both of us. Special thanks are due to my partner, Cathy DeGrandpre, who helped smooth the transition of ideas and liberate me from a "worried" writing style. In overcoming the challenges associated with writing as a team, we discovered a unique balance of style that rewards and delights us both. Without the collaboration of a writing partner and the element of teamwork, this paper would have fallen short of its potential and the reward would have been significantly less. I hope this proves true for you, the reader, as you continue with this text and gain insight into the contribution of women in the Roman era.

Adam Hrebeniuk

In many introductory undergraduate classes, students often write several short focused essays based on information gained through research during a term. These papers are often just three to four pages long and focus primarily on clear communication, logical organization of information in support of a tight thesis, and appropriate documentation. However, the process of research, drafting and writing is the same as it would be for a longer more complex assignment.

Paragraph 1
Paragraph one introduces the subject focus of the paper and moves quickly to the thesis. This paragraph also introduces the paper's clean, uncluttered prose style.

Some fields in the humanities continue to employ traditional footnotes, which are guided by the format set forth in the *Chicago Manual of Style*. Cathy and Adam have employed Chicago style for this history paper.

Superscript numerals (raised numbers like this[1]) follow the quotation or paraphrase in the text with no additional punctuation marks. The footnote begins with the same number. The first footnote for a source contains all of the usual citation information--author, title, place of publication, publisher, date. For any subsequent notes on a particular source that do not directly follow one another, the author's name and the page number are sufficient. If the same source is used for the very next note, the abbreviation, Ibid. may be used with the new page number or by itself if both the page and author are the same.

Some instructors will also permit students to cluster all of the notes on a page at the end of the paper under the heading, " Notes," which is placed immediately prior to the "Works Cited" page. With the exception of their location, footnotes and endnotes are the same.

Follow these general guidelines for footnotes:
- Indent the first line of each note 5 spaces, number the note followed by a period, begin the note, return to the left margin for succeeding lines
- Single-space the notes and double-space between the notes
- Number the notes consecutively throughout the paper
- Separate the notes from the text by a triple-space or a 12-space line beginning at the left

Paragraph 2
This paragraph focuses on the laws which were used to reinforce what were considered appropriate roles for women in ancient Rome and introduces the metaphor "she worked in wool" for the woman who maintained the home. The writers will return to this concept in the conclusion to the paper, providing a sense of unity.

Cathy DeGrandpre and
Adam Hrebeniuk
History 112
Professors Kathie Hunt and Dale Haefer
October, 1998

Contributions of Women during the Roman Era

During the Roman Era a woman's most common and socially acceptable roles were that

of *matrona* (or housewife) and priestess. Women who were slaves and peasants and thus unable

to achieve such status often became prostitutes. These are the limits in which women moved in

Roman Society. If a woman desired to take on a traditional male position, she was "acting

contrary to her culture's role for her and was subject to the severest criticism and punishment."[1]

Although these traditional roles inhibited women's direct participation in society and politics,

women still made significant contributions to Roman culture from within the confines of those

roles.

There were laws that rewarded and institutionalized the constraints placed on women,

especially laws that made a woman subordinate to her husband and the household. For example,

the father could emancipate sons from the restriction of *paterfamilias*, the absolute ownership of

the family. However, the only women who could become legally emancipated from the

paterfamilias were of the priestess class, Vestal Virgin.[2] As a housewife, a woman's duties were

strictly confined to having legitimate children and staying home to tend to the household. She

also supervised the slaves and performed "traditional labor such as spinning and making wool."[3]

These duties became so expected from women that they were repeatedly referred to in Roman

---

1. Bonnie S. Anderson and Judith P. Zinsser, *A History of Their Own: Volume I* (New York: Harper & Row, 1989), 42.

2. Sarah B. Pomeroy, *Goddesses, Whores, Wives, and Slaves: Women in Classical Antiquity* (New York: Schocken Books, 1995), 150.

3. Anderson, 40.

Paragraphs 3-4
This paragraph marks the beginning of the discussion of how some women used roles that were on the surface without power as a platform to influence. Cathie and Adam are using a strategy of enumerating a variety of causes and effects as they move through their discussion.

epitaphs with statements such as, "She kept the house and worked in wool."[4] Women of poorer

classes without dowries not only had to take care of their children and manage the household, but

also had to bring in an income. This was known as "double burden." A woman who felt this

double burden might sell food, clothing, or trinkets; she might offer food and lodging, manage a

brothel, or engage in prostitution.[5]

Prostitutes were socially condemned and had virtually no rights (they could not be

Christian or marry freeborn Roman men). However, many women rose to power through this

avenue and impacted Roman society.[6] According to Anderson, "A clever woman in the right

circumstances could turn her sexual connection with an important man into a secure and even

powerful future."[7] One woman who impacted Roman culture in this way was Theodora, who

rose from a prostitute to Empress of the Roman Empire in the East. Through an adulterous

relationship with an administrative official in Egypt, Theodora was able to meet men of the

highest level of society, including the Roman Emperor, Justinian, whom she eventually married.

In order to marry Theodora, Justinian had to amend the law that prohibited free men from

marrying prostitutes. Justinian eventually described Theodora as "partner in my deliberations,"

giving Theodora the power to strongly influence political policy.[8]

---

4.   Ibid., 41.

5.

6.   Ibid.

6.   Georges Duby, Michelle Perot and Pauline Schmitt Pantel, *A History of Women, I: From Ancient Goddesses to Christian Saints* (Cambridge, MA: Harvard University Press, 1992), 332.

7.   Anderson, 47.

8.   Ibid.

Paragraphs 5-6
The paragraph opens with a transition from the discussion of prostitutes and moves to priestesses. The writers help the reader anticipate the next point of development by pulling both ideas together in the opening sentence of the paragraph. Paragraph 6 adds details about Vestal Virgins.

Throughout the paper Adam and Cathy skillfully insert quotations directly into their sentences rather than always using introductory phrases such as *Pomeroy states that*.... When writers are able to simply incorporate a quote, sentences flow more smoothly.

Rather than denying her past as a prostitute, Theodora became a role model for women who, otherwise, believed that they could not rise above their circumstances. Theodora used her position to help women who turned to prostitution. She began a convent for former prostitutes and bought girls who had been sold into prostitution, freed them and provided for their future. Theodora also passed legislation that gave women more property rights and cleaned up the brothels.[9] Through her role as prostitute, Theodora was able to achieve a position that ultimately helped most women in Roman society.

The power gained through prostitution by women was seen as "undermin[ing] the hard-won status of the virginal daughter and the chaste wife."[10] To discourage this, the Roman government emphasized the value of religious cults that centered on chastity and familial bonds. Women may have been influenced by the cults to be more chaste; however, participating in them became another way for women to move beyond their traditional roles and have influence on Roman law. Two of the most influential priestly classes were the priestesses of Ceres and the Vestal Virgins. The priestesses of Ceres were the only women, besides Vestals, allowed a high priestly prominence. Ceres was the goddess of marriage, and the cult was exclusively in the hands of women.[11] The priestesses of Ceres encouraged the creation of laws that promoted the protection and, eventually, the freedom of women.

Another powerful priestess class was that of the Vestal Virgins. Six Vestals "…enrolled between the ages of six and ten, were obliged to remain virgins" and stoke the sacred

---

9. Ibid.

10. Ibid., 45.

11. Pomeroy, 215.

Paragraphs 7- 8
In these paragraphs, Cathy and Adam move to contributions based on personal wealth and artistic talents. At this point the writers emphasize not only the expansion of roles for contemporary Roman women, but also the lasting contributions that affected European women in later centuries. The selection of the order of their examples creates a unified discussion that moves logically from the power of a single individual to the collective impact on women across time and place.

"flame that symbolized the continuity of both family and community."[12] Even though the

Vestals were extremely regulated, they had more freedoms than any other women in Rome. The

Vestals were legally emancipated and were freed from the power of *paterfamilias*. Vestals were

the only women allowed to drive through the city of Rome in a two-wheeled wagon, a distinction

which was usually reserved for magistrates, high priests, and men of high office; they were also

the only women who "retained places on the imperial podium."[13] Seeing the priestesses enjoy

such liberties, aristocratic women wished to have the same elevated prestige and were eventually

granted the "rights of Vestals," which then led to their emancipation from the ownership of their

fathers or husbands. Since upper class women were now able to gain these privileges without the

vow of chastity, there were fewer Vestal candidates to choose from, which in turn created new

opportunities to daughters of lower class families to enroll as priestesses.[14] By exhibiting the

freedoms allowed to them, the Vestal Virgins inspired Roman women to seek greater freedoms

for themselves.

Women also gained freedoms and made contributions to society with their wealth. On

occasion, economic and political situations allowed wealth to come into the hands of women,

and after an eventual change in Roman law, daughters and wives were allowed an inheritance.

Many women used their wealth to become public benefactors. They made contributions such as

"constructing and endowing public buildings: meeting halls, temples, and baths."[15] Recognition

of a woman's creations and endowments was often carved in stone and publicly displayed so as

---

12. Ibid., 210.

13. Ibid., 214.

14. Ibid.

15. Anderson, 60.

Paragraph 9
In this concluding paragraph, the writers briefly summarize the main points of the essay. Since the essay is short and developed with a clear simple structure, a stronger conclusion might have included more attention to the lasting impact of Roman women in various contemporary spheres.

Overall Comment
As Adam points out in his "Writing Process" essay, the biggest challenge he faced in writing this paper was to learn how to work successfully as a team. He and Cathy had to work out many differing viewpoints as they made decisions on what to write about, how to share the research task, and most importantly, how to write in a single voice. They have adopted a direct clear style as a solution to the latter problem.

be remembered and "perhaps empower other women."[16]

Wealth also allowed women to pursue an education. Educated women influenced art, literature, philosophy and science. One such woman, Iaia of Cyzicus, was a celebrated painter in her time and had such a great talent that the price of her paintings was twice that of her contemporaries. Although none of these women's art survived, "the tradition they established of women working the arts endured in later European centuries."[17] This was also true of literature. Cornelia and Agrippina wrote letters and memoirs, and Sulpicia, a daughter of Cicero's friend was a poet.[18] The tradition of writing continued with these women and the women who followed them which "was one of the traditions inherited which most empowered European women in the centuries to come."[19] Through wealth women were able to move away from the duties of the housewife and directly impact Roman culture.

From these examples of women such as Theodora and the priestesses and from the influence of educated women and women benefactors, Roman women were able to expand their contributions to society and politics. Women no longer just made wool; they formed laws and moved about in society more freely. They became emancipated and inherited wealth and they impacted art, literature and science. Although limited by a confining social structure, Roman women gradually expanded the perimeters of their influence, which changed the future for the subsequent generations of European women.

---

16. Ibid.

17. Ibid., 61.

19. Anderson, 66.

Documentation Format

The paper illustrates the use of Chicago style footnotes for the citations with a "Works Cited" page.

Because all of the citation information is included in the initial footnote, some instructors do not require a Works Cited page. Be sure to find out what your instructor prefers. If you need to include a Bibliography (all sources that contributed to your thinking) or a "Works Cited" page (only the sources specifically cited in the paper), use the following guidelines:

- Separate the title from the first entry with a triple-space
- Begin each entry flush with the left margin; indent all subsequent lines 5 spaces
- Alphabetize the list according to the author's last name
- Single-space within, double-space between entries

Font and Layout

This paper has been word-processed using a 12-point Times New Roman font. The use of word processing software has greatly simplified the task of including footnotes because the computer will keep track of which notes to place on which pages for you. The manuscript is double-spaced with one-inch margins, flush left and ragged right justified. The header contains the writer's last name and the page number. It is located flush with the right margin, one half inch from the top right corner of each page.

Works Cited

Anderson, Bonnie S., and Judith P. Zinsser. *A History of Their Own: Volume I.* New York: Harper & Row, 1989.

Duby, Georges, Michelle Perot, and Pauline Schmitt Pantel. *A History of Women, I: From Ancient Goddesses to Christian Saints.* Cambridge, MA: Harvard University Press, 1992.

Ferrer, Guglielmo. *The Women of the Caesars.* New York: Loring and Mussey, 1911.

Pomeroy, Sarah B. *Goddesses, Whores, Wives, and Slaves: Women in Classical Antiquity.* New York: Schocken Books, 1995.

Process Writing for "Theories of Gender Differences in Visual-Spatial Abilities: A Critique"

When I first began this assignment, which was to read and respond to the major theories about an issue, I tried to figure out how I would organize the paper. I didn't know what format to put it in, so I just read tons and tons of research. I found the main theorists, read their studies and articles, and took lots of notes. I thought that by accumulating information an organization would suggest itself to me. Unfortunately, this is not exactly what happened.

When I began researching, I thought that there was a difference in men's and women's spatial abilities. I expected that all I'd have to do is present each theorist's study and describe why there was a difference between men and women. However, as I read the theories, I discovered that the theorists disagreed on key points about methods or conclusions. In addition, there seemed to be a problem with every study. I just had a feeling each study was flawed in some way-they overlooked this or that, or they over generalized. I was getting more and more worried about how I'd present these theories in my paper.

Finally, though, I came across a researcher who discredited all of the previous theories. I was surprised but relieved that he had had the same reaction to those theories as I had. Reading that researcher helped me come up with a way to organize my paper. I decided to categorize the theories, describe the theories in each category and then compare the categories, pointing out their flaws. Once I had this plan, the only problem I had in writing the paper was in deciding what information to include and what to leave out. I had done almost too much research looking up all the other studies that the main studies referred to. It was a bit frustrating to have everyone discrediting everyone else, because I felt I had to account for everything in the paper.

I learned a lot by doing this paper. It changed my views on gender differences. I came to the conclusion that gender differences probably don't exist, or at least don't exist in the way the theorists say they exist. The theorists I researched couldn't see what we know now, that their methods were gender-biased. When the biases are removed from the research methods, women tend to do as well or better than men on spatial tests.

Tami Kyle

Theories of Gender Differences in Visual-Spatial Abilities:

A Critique

by

Tami Kyle

English 1123

Professor Mark Shipman

December 12, 1992

Abstract

In general, the abstract is a brief summary of the content of an essay. Tami begins her abstract with the main purpose of her paper. She follows this sentence with a summary of the paper's basic structure and content.

176

Abstract

This paper explores the question of whether there are gender differences in human visual-spatial abilities. The paper proceeds by evaluating prior research on this issue in four areas: genetic theories, brain-lateralization theories, maturation rate theories, and hormone theories. Most earlier era research assumes that males possess superior visual-spatial abilities to females. However, this paper concludes that many of these earlier studies have suffered from such problems as poor control of variables and researcher bias.

Introduction

Tami begins by defining "spatial ability," a necessary step if she wants her lay readers to be able to understand her. Since she is writing to a broad audience of general readers rather than to experts in the field, she needs to include definitions of terms and summaries of research, and to exclude technical jargon.

Paragraph 2

Tami succinctly describes the central issue in spatial-ability research. This paragraph is similar to the abstract in that it lays out for the reader the basic direction and goal of the paper.

Paragraph 3

Tami uses subheads to help guide her readers through her paper. The purpose of this "menu" paragraph is to tell the readers what they can expect in the next few pages.

Tami uses the Council of Biology Editors (CBE) style to document her paper. The 1994 CBE guide style uses in-text parenthetical citations of two types. In general biological studies, the name-year system is preferred. In applied and medical science papers, the citation-sequence system is used. Tami has chosen the latter format and uses numerals rather than authors' names, however, and also includes a comma and the abbreviation "p." The order that the sources are referred to in the text determines their order on the "References" page; the first source cited is "1" the second "2," and so on.

While page numbers are not required unless the citation follows a direct quotation, Tami has added them to her citations. Note the comma after the reference number, the lower case *p.* preceding page numbers.

Theories of Gender Differences in Visual-Spatial Abilities: A Critique

Introduction

Visual-spatial abilities involve a person's ability to reason through form, distance, and space relationships. In other words, these abilities allow humans to orient themselves to a space by looking at it. All humans have these abilities to some extent: without them we could not walk down a sidewalk without falling down. But these abilities also come in degrees; people with superior visual-spatial abilities can often orient themselves in directions without looking at a compass. Superior visual-spatial abilities can also allow humans greater success in areas such as athletics, that require participants to make quick decisions regarding their orientation on the field, the floor, or the court.

Until the last decade it had been widely accepted that males possessed superior visual-spatial abilities when compared to females. However, current research has questioned this assumption's validity. Part of the weakness in these gender difference assertions lies in the fact that methods used in previous research that yielded supporting evidence of visual-spatial superiority among males were often faulty and did not attempt to account for other variables that had an effect on the outcomes of the studies. In addition, recent research reveals that these perceived gender differences in visual-spatial abilities have lessened over time, which indicates that environmental rather than innate factors may be the contributing cause of differences. Additionally, gender biases on the part of the previous researchers may have contributed to the early findings that purported to show male superiority. This paper examines and evaluates claims made by both previous and more recent research into the visual-spatial issue.

Four Recent Basic Theories

Researchers of visual-spatial superiority often begin their studies by choosing a particular theory of why sex-related differences exist and pursue their research on that theory (1, p. 789). Of the many theories that have been developed to account for these differences-, the four that are most often used are *genetic theory, brain lateralization theory, maturation rate theory* (2, p. 546), and *hormone theory* (3, p. 63).

Paragraph 4
With the structural pattern that she uses for all four theories, Tami begins her discussion here with a brief description of the theory.

Paragraph 5
Tami now points out the flaw in the genetic theory. The first half of her paragraph continues the summary of the theory, focusing on the testing conditions that must be present before the theory can be considered valid. Tami summarizes this part of the theory because it is the conditions that she specifically finds fault with. The transition sentence that begins "However" signals Tami's critique.

Paragraph 6
Tami continues the two-paragraph structure, the first paragraph summarizing the theory, the second pointing out the flaw(s) in the theory's assumptions and/or methods.

Genetic Theory

The genetic theory, the most widely accepted of the four (1, p. 790), rests on the idea that a recessive gene carried on the X chromosome is responsible for spatial perception. Due to the recessive nature of this trait on the X chromosome, a larger population of males was thought to possess the trait than females (4, p. 294), because the XX chromosome configuration in females would keep the trait in the recessive expression while the XY chromosome configuration of males would allow the recessive trait to be manifested.

While this assertion makes logical mathematical and genetic sense, several factors must be present for this hypothesis to be provable and repeatable. The conditions are that the scores on spatial-visualization tests should correspond between mothers and their sons because sons inherit the X chromosome from their mothers. These mother-son correspondences should also be higher than mother-daughter correspondences due to the recessive nature of the trait, and there should be no correlation between fathers' and sons' visual-spatial abilities. This lack of correlation would show that the trait is not carried on the Y chromosome, which sons get from their fathers. However, the theory has not maintained its credibility in studies designed to test this hypothesis. In fact, contradictory results were obtained. These experiments resulted in higher correlations between fathers and sons than between mothers and sons, which disproved the theory (1, p. 790). Furthermore, speculation is growing in the research community the spatial ability is probably also controlled by non-genetic factors such as the physical and social environment (1, p. 791).

Brain Lateralization Theory

The brain-lateralization theory is based on the belief that males are more dependent on the right side of their brains for problem solving; females are believed to be more reliant on the left side of their brains. According to some research, the right side of the brain is responsible for cognitive functions such as spatial visualization; therefore, males are thought to have the advantage in cognitive abilities (1, p. 791). While research done in efforts to prove this theory has turned up convincing evidence, the conclusions reached seem somewhat faulty.

Paragraph 7
Tami's critique of the brain lateralization theory is longer than her critique of the genetic theory because the brain lateralization theory is more complicated to describe. Unlike her discussion of the genetic theory, Tami devotes an entire paragraph to this second theory, and places her transition sentence at the end of paragraph 6.

Paragraph 9
Tami can keep her critique of the maturation rate theory short because the theory is similar to the previous theory's flaw.

Paragraph 10
This is a longer paragraph because the study being described is in two parts. Tami includes a short critique sentence ("These findings, however") after her description of the first part of the study to provide a pause in the paragraph.

182

Like other research used to support spatial-visualization superiority, studies conducted in support of brain-lateralization have utilized faulty methods. Take, for instance, studies in the 1970s which were based on test results of epilepsy patients who had their corpus callosurn severed to prevent seizures (1, p. 792). This separation of the hemispheres of the brain made it easier to determine the specialization of the two halves. However, evidence from this research could not be applied to the entire population. Clearly, the group being studied was not representative of normal functioning individuals and is not a reliable basis upon which to generalize; the test group may have had unique features present in their brains, due to the presence of nerve and chemical factors only present in persons with epilepsy, which would not be applicable to the general population (1, p. 792).

Maturation Rate Theory

Maturation rates are another factor upon which supposed visual-spatial differences have been based (5, p. 29). In maturation rate theory, researchers believed that regardless of sex, "late maturers perform better on spatial tasks" (5, p. 30). To test this hypothesis, male and female participants were separated into two groups—one for late maturers and one for early maturers. These groups were further divided into groups by age. Tests measuring visual-spatial ability were administered to each group and yielded results that supported the maturation hypothesis (5, p. 34).

Here again, however, the test results must be questioned due to weaknesses in testing methods. While it may be true that supporting evidence was found, this experiment failed to recognize other significant variables such as diet, heredity, and environment that probably affected the results. As difficult as it may be, studies cannot be considered viable unless they account for every variable which might have an effect on the outcome of the research.

Hormone Theory

Still another theory of sex-related differences is that sex hormones affect the level of spatial ability (3, p. 63). Research by Kimura to support this theory relied on differential experience. Kimura used research concluding that men who reached puberty at a later than normal age had low levels of testosterone

Paragraph 11

Tami has to use a necessary technical term, "estradiol," but she follows the term with a dependent clause defining it.

Paragraph 12

Tami begins the main part of her paper, which focuses on the differences between earlier, faulted studies and more recent and more valid studies. Notice, though, that even though Tami seems to divide studies by time periods (before vs. after the late 1980s), she is not saying that any study before the late 1980s is "bad," and any study later is "good." What she finds at fault are the assumptions and methods of the studies, which is a much more sophisticated approach than taking issue with the time periods of particular studies.

Paragraphs 13 - 15

Tami describes two studies that begin to refute the idea that gender differences exist in spatial ability. These paragraphs constitute a transitional section between the discussion of the four basic theories that assume there is a gender difference and the theories that openly refute this assumption. Tami sees the two studies mentioned here as moving in the right direction, but still as problematic in their assumptions.

and poor scores on visual-spatial tests. These men's scores were compared with scores of men who had reached

puberty at a normal age, but at the time of testing had lower testosterone levels due to disease. These studies showed

lower test scores among the males whose testosterone level was the result of later maturity. These findings,

however, do not necessarily lead to a reliable conclusion due to the narrowness of the test groups. Kimura then tried

to support her point with an experiment with rats. In this study, rats were placed in a maze to determine their

"spatial-problem solving abilities." It found that female rats used both geometric and landmark cues to find their

way thorough the maze, while males only relied on geometric cues. When the male rats were castrated, they began

to rely on landmark cues, just as female rats had previously done.

Though this evidence seems to support the theory, these studies did not account for the fact that testosterone has

been found to be converted into estradiol in the brain, which could aid in the determination of spatial ability (3, p.

64). Because this factor was not examined, the information obtained and the conclusion drawn by Kimura can only

be considered partially valid.

Comparisons of Past and Recent Studies

As seen in several past studies that concentrated on sex-related visual-spatial differences, failure to represent all

variables is a major shortcoming. With few exceptions, studies conducted prior to the late 1980s found visual-spatial

sex-related differences present. However, even these studies recognized, as previously mentioned, that without

taking adequate measures to control situational variables, a concrete conclusion can not be drawn. Recent studies

that have more accurately controlled all variables have tended to conclude that sex-related spatial-visual differences

are few or nonexistent. In one 1990 study, gender differences were responsible for no more than 5% of the variances

in the test scores, while situational variables were held accountable for more than 20% (6, p. 543). Comparing other

examples of previous studies with more recent ones, which utilized different methods and included various

situational factors, shows that the theory of visual-spatial differences between genders seems to be weak.

A study conducted in 1977 by Eisenburg and McGinty employed a multiple-choice exam which contained

twenty-seven items in an effort to measure the visual-spatial abilities of the subjects tested (7, p. 100). The subjects

for the study were university students who were enrolled in four mathematics courses including calculus, business

statistics, remedial mathematics, and mathematics for elementary school teachers. The purpose of this study was to

determine if there was a marked sex difference in spatial abilities of individuals with the same career goals (7, p.

99). After comparing their findings, Eisenburg and McGinty arrived at "mixed results" (7, p. 101). In their studies,

Paragraph 13
Notice that Tami does not naively or wholeheartedly endorse the studies that she thinks are more valid than the previous ones discussed. She finds a problem even with the study by Eisenburg and McGinty. Still, her preferences in favor of this study are apparent by her rather mild criticism in comparison to her criticism of the previous studies. She might have found a more serious flaw in this study had her focus been different

Paragraph 14
Tami moves on to a second study that refutes the earlier research.

Paragraph 15
Again, although Tami finds this study more valid than others, she also is aware of flaws in its assumptions and testing methods. Pointing out these flaws does not hurt her own position; indeed, it tends to support it because it makes Tami appear to be a thorough and critical, rather than a naive, reader.

females received higher scores in all groups except the teacher group. Still, because of their results, they concluded that "there are some sex differences in regard to spatial abilities." However, their report is faulty because they failed to mention that these "sex differences" were in favor of the females in most cases (7, p. 103). This omission continued the research community's acceptance of a less than credible theory.

In yet another study conducted in 1977, the continued assumption was made that sex-related spatial-visual differences exist despite the findings of research (8, p. 294). The purpose of this study was to determine how training, such as playing with trucks and blocks as opposed to playing with dolls, affects the visual-spatial differences between males and females. The belief, at that time, was that the blocks and trucks familiarized males with geometric shapes and led to their higher scores than females on visual-spatial exams. Females, on the other hand, were not considered to be as familiar with geometric shapes because they were assumed to play more with non-angular toys such as dolls. To conduct the study, one hundred and thirty-three children were placed randomly in either a control group or one of two training groups. Of the two training groups, children in one group were given previous exposure to a complicated picture that contained a diamond shape which was to be identified. This previous exposure was designed to correlate to the previous exposure males receive from blocks and trucks. The other group was simply asked to identify the geometric shape without the exposure. The third group, the control group, conversed with experimenters and was given no instruction in identifying the diamond shaped geometric object. Each group was then assessed according to the children's abilities to identify the diamond shape and the amount of time the identification took.

The findings were that males showed no improved identification of the diamond shape when given previous exposure. On the other hand, females showed a marked improvement with the aid of previous exposure (8, p. 293). According to the researchers, this meant that the lower scores of females can be attributed to lack of confidence. This is supported because females, when given confidence through previous exposure, were more able to identify the diamond shape (8, p. 294). Though this experiment did attempt to research environmental situations which affect visual-spatial differences, it neglected to determine whether the assumed sex-related differences actually existed. The researchers approached the study with the assumption that the sexes were different in their abilities, and the evidence supported that assumption. However, had the methods of research also included examination of the differences caused by environmental factors along with studying the variance between the sexes, the results may

Paragraph 16
Tami now begins to present the studies she finds most valid. She ends paragraph 15 with a transitional sentence to set up this section.

Paragraph 17
Tami saves the study by Feingold, Haldane, and Mitchell, the study that helped Tami determine a process and organization for her paper, for last. Because she aligns herself most closely with this study, she feels more comfortable presenting its findings as the "last word" on the topic. Since this study is not only by Feingold, but by two other researchers as well, Tami needs to acknowledge the collaborative effort rather than referring only to "Feingold... he." She could use the abbreviation "Feingold et al." and "they" after she has initially acknowledged them.

have been totally different. In fact, more current research has indicated that visual-spatial differences between males and females are not even sufficient enough to warrant study.

By contrast to these older studies, several recent ones find little support for gender differences in visual-spatial ability. One study investigated the relationship of gender differences to schooling, location, and chronological age (6, p. 535). Research in this study involved 1,115 Peruvian children, who were in the first, second, and third grades or were unschooled (6, p. 5). Each child was given a total of 16 tests in which cognitive abilities, including spatial-visualization, was a measured factor (6, p. 535). The results of the study led the researchers to conclude that there was "little support" for the idea that "boys possess greater quantitative and spatial skills than girls" (6, p. 546). In fact, this study found that no more than 5% of scoring variations were due to gender differences. It did, however, show that 20% of the variance was due to other background factors such as schooling, location, and age (6, p. 543). This study also found evidence that indicates that increased schooling, which leads to more shared common experiences, decreased the gender differences (6, p. 547).

Other evidence suggesting gender differences are not as significant as once believed was found in another recent study in which sex-related differences were noted to have decreased over the years of research (9, p. 95). The study of the results of tests which were conducted from 1947 until recent years by Feingold has shown that the differences accounted for in the earlier tests were no longer found in more recent studies (9, p. 95). Feingold did discover that males scored higher on such tests as "Mechanical Reasoning" and "Space Relations," which supported the ideas of the past that males possess superior visual-spatial abilities than females. However, as Feingold began to examine the tests which were conducted over the years, he found that "girls ... have closed the gap" on many of the tests in which males had previously been superior. He also found that the differences in scores of males and females on "Mechanical Reasoning" and "Space Relations" tests had been reduced by half in recent tests (9, p. 101). In trying to explain these differences, Feingold postulated that the sex biases which seemed to be factors in the tests administered in previous years have recently been removed. The less biased assumptions and approaches of the more recent researchers—if Feingold's assertion is correct—would certainly account for the more even scores of males and females in current tests (9, p. 102).

Conclusion

In her conclusion, Tami summarizes the critique rather than the review-of-theories section of the paper in order to emphasize her opinion, rather than the content, of the theories.

Overall Comment

Tami's paper illustrates a sophisticated approach to a common assignment. The organizational pattern of summary and critique is a fairly simple one to follow, but Tami goes further and employs it in a complex way. She categorizes the theories, then includes a summary and critique of each category. In addition, she does not present the theories in any cut and dried way, but tries to show that they each have valid and invalid elements.

The paper also shows a clear awareness of audience. Tami never gets too technical, but neither does she oversimplify the issues or condescend to her readers. She treats her readers as intelligent people who will understand the implications of her critique.

Finally, Tami strikes a balance between formality and informality in her tone. Though she does not use "I," she avoids the dry formality of "one" by a careful choice of words that allows her to avoid having to use either pronoun. The tone is informal yet scholarly.

Conclusion

All too often, research that is printed in a scientific journal automatically receives the "halo effect" of authority, and therefore is considered to be correct. This is magnified when the theory being supported, such as the idea that males possess better visual-spatial abilities than females, is widely supported by society. In such a case, the reader may overlook the faults of the research, such as failure to account for situational variables, the validity of the factors involved, and the misrepresentation of facts as well as gender biases of test methods. These situations were all present in past studies of sex-related visual-spatial differences; however, this theory was still considered viable until recent research brought about new ideas. Hopefully, in the future, individuals will look at the whole picture presented and will see that more facts are represented to disprove the male visual-spatial superiority than are presented to prove it and will study research findings with a more critical eye so misinterpretations of information do not continue to stymie our understanding of the human species.

Documentation Format

Tami uses one of the two citation styles recommended by the Council of Biology Editors (CBE) documentation system, The sources quoted within the paper are included on a "References" page. Use the following general rules as a guide in formatting this page:

- Center the heading "References".
- Double-space all lines.
- Sources are listed and numbered according to the order they appeared in the paper itself. They are not alphabetized in the citation-sequence system.
- Spell out last names, but only use initials for authors' first names. All authors' names are listed last name first, then initials. For works with more than one author, use commas to separate authors' names.

Font and Layout

Tami produced this document on a home computer in 10-point Times font, using the font's italics where needed. The manuscript is double-spaced, with one-inch margins, flush left, ragged right.

References

1. Caplan PJ, MacPherson GM, Tobin P. Do sex-related differences in spatial abilities exist? American Psychologist 1985;40:786-97.

2. Goldstein D, Haldane D, Mitchell C. Sex differences in visual-spatial ability: the role of performance factors. Memory and Cognition 1990;18:546-50.

3. Kimura D. How sex hormones boost-or cut-intellectual ability. Psychology Today 1989 Nov:63-6.

4. Sherman JA. Problem of sex differences in space perception and aspects of intellectual functioning. Psychological Review 1967;74:290-9.

5. Waber DP. Sex differences in mental abilities, hemispheric lateralization, and rate of physical growth at adolescence. Developmental Psychology 1977;13 (1):29-38.

6. Stevenson HW. Influences of schooling and urban-rural residence on gender differences in cognitive abilities and academic achievement. Sex Roles 1990; 23:535-50.

7. Connor JM, Serbin LA, Schackman M. Sex differences in children's training on a visual-spatial test. Developmental Psychology 1977;13(3):293-4.

8. Eisenberg TA, McGinty RL. On spatial visualization in college students. The Journal of Psychology 1977; 95:99-100.

9. Feingold D, Haldane D, Mitchell C. Cognitive gender differences in visual-spatial ability: the role of performance factors. Memory and Cognition 1990;18(5):546-50.